D0442051

Decisions of
ROBERT S. McNAMARA

Decisions of ROBERT S. McNAMARA

A Study of the Role of the Secretary of Defense

by James M. Roherty

University of Miami Press
Coral Gables, Florida

Designed by Bernard Lipsky
Manufactured in the United States of America

Permissions to quote were generously granted by:
Atheneum Publishers, for material from Emmet J. Hughes,
The Ordeal of Power, copyright 1962 and copyright 1963;
Doubleday & Company, Inc., for material from
Dwight D. Eisenhower, *The White House Years,* Volume 1,
Mandate for Change, 1953-1956, copyright 1963;
Harvard University Press, for material from Samuel P. Huntington,
The Soldier and the State, copyright 1967,
and from Charles J. Hitch and Roland N. McKean,
The Economics of Defense in the Nuclear Age, copyright 1960;
and Rand McNally & Co., for material from Davis B. Bobrow, ed.,
Components of Defense Policy, copyright 1965,
and from Edward S. Quade, ed.,
Analysis for Military Decisions, copyright 1964.

For Lewis F. Roherty and Ralph H. Mitchell

Contents

Acknowledgments

In recent years a number of studies have appeared which provide important perspectives on the making of national security policy. The present work was undertaken because it seemed to me that in these studies not enough attention was directed to the very critical role of the Secretary of Defense. What is most needed at this juncture is a series of monographs (looking ultimately to a comprehensive study) on the transformation of the office of the Secretary of Defense and, indeed, the national security policy process itself. In the immediate aftermath of the historic term of Robert S. McNamara, such studies will necessarily be partial in scope as well as tentative in conclusions. Yet at the same time they must be undertaken if the important enterprise of "theory" is not to lag behind "accumulated practice."

Two works by Samuel Huntington, *The Soldier and the State* (Cambridge, 1957) and *The Common Defense* (New York, 1961), Paul Hammond's *Organizing for Defense* (Princeton, 1961), and the more recent study by John Ries, *The Management of Defense* (Baltimore, 1965), provide a broad overview of the development of the defense structure up to 1961. Professor John Masland, in a review of the Ries study (*American Political Science Review,* June 1965), points out that what is needed is an extension of these kinds of analyses into the McNamara administration of the Department of Defense. Jack Raymond, formerly of *The New York*

Times, has touched briefly on the McNamara period (*Power at the Pentagon,* New York, 1964). This is a useful book but it does not look to the development of "theory." In their reviews of William Kaufmann's *The McNamara Strategy* (New York, 1964), Bernard Brodie (*World Politics,* July 1965) and S. L. A. Marshall (*United States Naval Institute Proceedings,* March 1965), whose credentials in the field of defense studies do not need to be attested, emphasize the necessity for a scholarly rather than polemical assessment of the McNamara tenure. To date it is safe to say that some of the most trenchant analyses of the administration of national security have come from experienced military commentators in the press (Hanson Baldwin, S. L. A. Marshall, and so forth) and, indeed, from the Pentagon reporters of the New York and Washington papers particularly. One must concur with Professor Arnold Rogow (*Political Science Quarterly,* June 1965) that political scientists concerned with civil-military relations theory recognize their indebtness to these significant sources.

An important source of data and analyses, the value of which, again, is perhaps not sufficiently appreciated, is the admittedly voluminous product of congressional committees. There is little question that a vast amount of candid testimony and hard substance is to be mined from the hearings and reports of these committees. Indeed, this is a source to be preferred over two others for precise information and comprehensive coverage, namely, personal interviews and direct releases from the Department of Defense. The work of the Subcommittee on National Policy Machinery (the Jackson Subcommittee) of the Senate Government Operations Committee, the Defense Subcommittee of the House Appropriations Committee, and the House Armed Services Committee is cited as the most valuable of committee hearings. The reports of "outside" agencies engaged in defense research offer another source of material. The biographies and memoirs of key figures in the postwar formulation of American security are yet another. The amount of material available is striking; it is a more than adequate base for the general reconstruction of civil-military theory.

The task of acknowledging debts that have accrued in the writing of this book is a pleasant one. The financial assistance of the College of William and Mary and the Institute of Social Science Research was indispensable. Those who have read the manuscript in various stages of evolution have been more than generous. I am particularly indebted to Robert Connery, Martin Clancy, Brewster Denny, Thomas K. Glennan, Jr., John Lovell, Aaron Wildavsky, James Schlesinger, Mose Harvey, Clyde Wooten, Major Ralph Hoffmann, USAF, and Earl Voss. I am most grateful to the last named for his encouragement and perception. There is also a special debt to persons unnamed. I want to take note of students who have been not only helpful but a source of encouragement as well: my thanks go to Albert Eldridge, Patsy Dickinson, Wilford Kale, and Robert Trice. Mrs. Claire Buckle and Mrs. Gretchen English have been the model typists, startlingly patient. Maxine continues to be the model wife. I hold none of the above accountable for what follows.

Williamsburg, Virginia
January 1970

The Secretaries of Defense

Name	Appointed
James V. Forrestal	September 1947
Louis A. Johnson	April 1949
George C. Marshall	September 1950
Robert A. Lovett	October 1951
Charles E. Wilson	January 1953
Neil H. McElroy	October 1957
Thomas S. Gates, Jr.	December 1959
Robert S. McNamara	January 1961
Clark M. Clifford *	March 1968
Melvin R. Laird *	January 1969

* Subsequent to the period covered in the present study

Decisions of
ROBERT S. McNAMARA

Introduction

 The focal point of civil-military relations in the United States since World War II has been the Secretary of Defense. For two decades attention has centered on the role of the Secretary of Defense in the national security policy apparatus. Nonetheless, it is still difficult to articulate precisely the role of the secretary. The "practice" of the nine men who have held the office does not lend itself to the formulation of a single role concept. [1] Clearly, Robert S. McNamara, who has had the longest tenure in a still young Department of Defense, has substantially affected any formulation that may be made of the role of the secretary. However, when Mr. McNamara came to the Pentagon in January 1961, a considerable body of precedent had been built up with respect to the definition of "the authority, direction, and control" of the Secretary of Defense. A body of "practical wisdom" had been produced by the men most intimately involved. Grappling with immediate, vital issues on a week-to-week basis in the formative years of the Department of Defense, these men reached conclusions which were a distillation of their firsthand experience and their innermost convictions. Explicit role concepts were not developed; there would be little time for the sustained, detached intellectual task of "theory." Yet they had reached conclusions, and it is the assumption of this writer that it is the conclusions of "the

men" which best define the role of the Secretary of Defense.
For the period 1947-1960 these conclusions can be presented in two formulations, the first of which prescribes a *generalist* role for the secretary and the second a *functionalist* role.[2] Chapter I traces the emergence of the two role concepts which constitute a point of departure for Mr. McNamara in 1961. The first conceptualization of the role of the Secretary of Defense is associated with what must surely be regarded as a singular group of men. These are the "Truman men": the Cold War Cadre—the *princepes* of postwar American internationalism (James V. Forrestal, Dean Acheson, William Draper, W. Averell Harriman, Robert A. Lovett, John J. McCloy, William Clayton, Dean Rusk, Thomas S. Gates, and others). Three served as Secretary of Defense (Forrestal, 1947-1949; Lovett; 1950-1952; Gates, 1959-1960), and they are most directly responsible for a generalist formulation. Two exceptional personages are most prominently the formulators of a distinct and opposed role for the Secretary of Defense, although neither served in that office. President Dwight D. Eisenhower and Governor Nelson A. Rockefeller must be credited with the basic thinking underlying a functionalist concept, and Secretaries of Defense Charles E. Wilson and Neil H. McElroy can be credited only in a secondary way.

Following an analysis of the "precedents," this study is concerned primarily with Secretary McNamara and his impact on the office. We shall attempt to determine which of the two role concepts Mr. McNamara most closely identified with and the degree to which he departed from either or both. I have selected for analysis two critical problem areas to which Mr. McNamara gave close attention during his term as secretary with a view to elucidating the connections between his decisions and the conceptual scheme of which they are the products. Out of this rather sharply delimited undertaking I have sought to point up issues which a new management system raises, issues that are of concern to the public administrator and the scholar. The first area, in broad terms, is the Strategic Forces. I am concerned with how Secretary McNamara thought about the wide spectrum of strategic scenarios and how he made specific decisions within this area. Consequently, the discussion in Chapter III focuses on the decision not to build an Advanced Manned Strategic Aircraft (AMSA) in the context, again, of the broad strategic equation. The second area is as wide as the span of the General Purpose Forces. The focus in Chapter IV is also on the secretary's relationships with one of the services—this time the Navy rather than the Air Force—and on the specific question of building a second, nuclear-powered aircraft carrier. The two case studies of the McNamara impact on the role of the Secretary of Defense are preceded by a discussion of the intellectual premises of "the new management" in Chapter II.

The most significant result of the present study might be the evidence that it provides for the continuing depoliticization of public policy. In the Department of Defense during the course of the 1960s, in spite of the existence of a tradition to the contrary, the displacement of political prudence and political process by technical rationality and the processes of the functionary made its farthest advance. At the center of what is an unmistakably radical development is Robert S. McNamara, the eighth Secretary of Defense. His understanding of the role of the secretary is not only critical for the national security policy process; its impact on public policy as a whole is profound. Mr. McNamara is not to be criticized for his cast of mind; what is subject to critical analysis is the attempt to reconstruct the order of policy, strategy, resources, and operations to conform to this cast of mind.

It is seldom contended that politics and technology are not separate endeavors and, indeed, that politics is not primary. But if the distinction is to be maintained and the primacy of politics is to be guaranteed, the distinction must be explicit. The absence of an understanding of politics has given rise to efforts to fuse the processes of politics and technology in the names of science and system. Political process assumes diverse and legitimate interests; consequently, effort is directed not at overcoming or transcending those interests but at evolving a continuing series of conciliations. Conciliation is the product of political prudence, not of rationalized techniques. That is to say that the politician makes choices or judgments within a given value frame or in terms of a prevailing consensus as to how conflicting interests are to be reconciled. The politician refuses to decide on the basis of a single factor or technique; instead he considers a broad range of factors. His conclusion is the result of bargaining with a plurality of interests whose standing he recognizes and accepts. When efforts are made to resolve political process into technical process through the forging of new decision structures, the assumptions of politics are abandoned and the assumptions of technique are substituted. Political prudence and pluralistic bargaining are displaced by system—invariably a system capped by a single actor.[3] The thrust of technical process is twofold. It may be stated as follows: that more beneficial results (outcomes) in terms of an established standard of efficiency (economic) may be expected from rationalized procedures than from political process, and that ultimately a single actor relying on such a "system" can make more effective policy choices than can emerge from political process. Under the guise of making policy, the rationalization of technique displaces politics.

The phenomenon of "functionaries" taking flight from the "unorganized and incalculable realm" of politics and turning all "problems of politics into problems of administration" is an old one.[4] It is well known that the inclusive, pluralistic bargaining mode of policy formulation is antithetical to the exclusive processes of administrative decisions. The increasing technical rationalization of public policy is not a new finding of this study. What a study of the Secretary of Defense over the past two decades provides is some measure of the distance that today lies between a basically political understanding of the secretarial role (Forrestal-Lovett-Gates) and an apolitical understanding (McNamara). Mr. McNamara's role concept is apolitical not in the sense that it eschews policy in favor of an exclusive concern with "management" (Wilson-McElroy), but in the more significant sense that it subordinates policy to technical process. The ascendency of management and the decline of policy, the elaboration of structure and technique, and the faltering of innovation and bargaining mark the McNamara years. It is clear that while imagination and flexibility are vital in the determination of policy and strategy, the thrust of the new management has made for increasing rigidity. It is clear that while a creative, reenforcing tension between military and civilian professionalism is indispensable to national security policy, the thrust of the new management has been to neutralize such pluralism. The new management is, in a word, apolitical. As such it is a process in the context of American government that must be thoroughly reexamined.

It will be emphasized throughout that Secretary McNamara addressed the problems of his office and the central question of civilian control of the military through the modality of management. The major issues with which he had to cope were understood by him as functions of management and most readily resolved through a managerial process. Examination of Mr. McNamara's extensive "public transcript" reveals little in the way of a theoretical construct of the office of the Secretary of Defense. His conception of the role of the Secretary of Defense, his conception of the principle of civilian supremacy, derive to a significant degree from the contributions of others. The force of Mr. McNamara's administration of the Department of Defense was due in great part to a remarkable philosophical consistency between himself and important civilian subordinates. The secretary, with a renowned capacity to assimilate information and translate it into programs, must be credited with the "decisions" which put a new aspect on this office. But again, not all of the premises underlying these decisions are his.

The present study is put forward as a work in political theory; more specifically, it is an effort to contribute to a general theory of civil-military relations—an area still characterized by a paucity of theorizing. It does not, itself, offer a general theory of what Samuel P. Huntington has called "objective civilian control"; the undertaking is more limited in scope and complexity. As I have tried to suggest in the subtitle, it will be sufficient if this study does no more than enhance our understanding of the role of the Secretary of Defense. The evolution of this role since 1947 must be understood if the enterprise of maintaining a viable theory of civil-military relations is to go forward.

Tentative conclusions about the McNamara impact on the balance between civilians and military in the national security policy process suggest that conceptions of the role of the Secretary of Defense which arose prior to 1961 must now be modified. In Mr. McNamara's understanding and response to the problem of civilian control there are inevitable and important consequences for national security policy. The implications for strategic doctrine, force structure, the professional relationship between civilians and military, and, most importantly perhaps, responsible decision-making in large bureaucratic structures must occupy scholars for many years. Whether the tenure of Mr. McNamara in the Pentagon bodes well or ill for the long-term security of the nation cannot be decided at this juncture; what is clear, however, is that an understanding of his term as Secretary of Defense is indispensable. This is an accolade for any man.

1

Generalists and Functionalists

 The unification battle at the close of World War II had as its crux the recognition that appropriate civilian control of the military and the formulation and execution of national security policy would require arrangements quite distinct from those that prevailed during the war. It was impossible to contemplate the relationships which obtained among the President (Franklin Delano Roosevelt), the Joint Chiefs of Staff (JCS), and the civilian secretaries extending into the postwar period. President Truman was anxious to make the transition to peacetime procedures, although in his preoccupation with other issues he was determined not to lose sight of the principle of civilian supremacy in postwar defense arrangements. He was entirely disposed toward the suggestions being put forward by the Army as early as 1944. In certain respects the Army proposals sought to retain World War II presidential–JCS relationships. Plans advanced by General Joseph T. McNarney in 1944 and General J. Lawton Collins in 1945 would have put the wartime working relationships into institutional form. In the face of little enthusiasm for either plan, the JCS proposed a more modest alternative which amounted in effect to formalizing the World War II role of General George C. Marshall. This plan had as its key feature a single chief of staff who would report directly to the President. All of the plans envisaged a civilian secretary of the armed forces, but he was in Huntington's phrase "cut strictly along Stimsonian lines."[1] He would not be crucial in determination of policy, strategic plans, or budget. What the Joint Chiefs, and the Army in particular, had in mind was the traditional hierarchial General Staff concept—"a tightly structured pyramid under the direction of a powerful executive."[2] The reference in this instance is not to a civilian secretary but to a single chief of staff. What was contemplated was a powerful, uniformed executive standing between the President and the armed forces who would exercise the power of the President and maintain the principle of civilian supremacy. It did not seem incongruous to the JCS that this would be a military man, or that such a plan would tend to diminish the presidential role.[3]

James V. Forrestal

The Secretary of the Navy, James V. Forrestal, a man of modest physical presence, reticent, and burdened, struck one as constantly absorbed in thought. Dismayed and disturbed by the Army proposals, he dreaded the impending and inevitable struggle over the postwar structure of national security policy. His initial reaction was untypical, instinctive, and negative: did the Army not understand that by having a chief of staff report directly to the President, bypassing the secretary of the armed forces, they were placing a "military man" in the position to resolve or summarize disputes before they reached the President?[4] The plan was unconscionable on two grounds: it nullified the authority of the civilian secretary, and it put as final arbiter between the Navy and the President a military man who on most occasions would not be "Navy." Moreover, the plan raised the question of the identity and integrity of the Navy, indeed, of all the services. Forrestal enlisted the assistance of a colleague, Ferdinand Eberstadt, to head a Navy policy group which would bring forward proposals embodying two bedrock principles: the integral relationship of military policy and national policy, and the retention of separate services.[5]

In keeping with Forrestal's directive, the central theme of the Eberstadt Report[6] was integration of the totality of factors bearing on national security policy. Military policy, strictly construed, must be placed in the context of overall national policy. This had not been done adequately during World War II, and the Army proposals with their emphasis on administration were still begging this primary policy issue.

Both Forrestal and Eberstadt were familiar with, and by no means disenchanted with, the committee or board approach to integration and coordination. Committees would be the devices by which a federal coordination would be achieved in national security policy. The separate services under their respective civilian secretaries would retain effective operational control. The Joint Chiefs of Staff would remain intact. There would be no single chief nor, indeed, a chairman of the JCS. Neither Forrestal nor Eberstadt called for a single secretary of the armed forces; Eberstadt specifically questioned the feasibility of such a position. In their study, *Forrestal and the Navy,* Robert G. Albion and Robert H. Connery quote Forrestal on two occasions, first before the Woodrum Committee in 1944 and then in 1947 before the Senate Armed Services Committee on the National Security Act hearings. There is little doubt that Forrestal opposed as fundamentally unsound the proposal of a single department and a single secretary: "There is no human being capable, in my judgment, of sitting on top of all that and assuring that you have the fine integration and efficiency which it is presumed would result from that consolidation"; and, "It is my belief that in any field of human activity, whether it is business or government, there is a definite limit to the size of any administrative unit which can be successfully directed by any one man."[7]

Primary responsibility for the broad guidelines of national security policy would lie with the National Security Council.

Research and development, intelligence, economic and industrial mobilization, and atomic energy would lie with boards or commissions which, along with the Joint Chiefs, would report directly to the President. John Ries comments on this approach, which was directly opposed to the Army's hierarchical concept: "It assured the President that all major issues would come directly to him for decisions. But along with this, it assured the President that the issues would be brought by those who had the responsibility to implement the decision once it was made . . . just as important, information on these issues was brought from different sources with different points of view."[8] Forrestal consciously sought to rely on the merits of a measure of "disorder" at lower levels; the structure would not stand or fall on its organizational symmetry. He saw the problem as one of blending a pluralism of professional talents; it would be all important who the men were. Nonetheless, it was quickly recognized that the apex of the structure did pose problems. The problem of a "principal assistant" to the President could not be begged if only because the Army had a specific answer for it.

It needs to be emphasized that up to this point Forrestal was not addressing himself to the problem of a single department, much less a single secretary. His concern stemmed from a preoccupation with the future of the Navy and the Marine Corps. The future of naval aviation was in jeopardy from enthusiasts of "autonomous air power." The World War II achievements of naval aviation, however, had impressed on Forrestal the validity of a separate fleet air arm; likewise, the unique capabilities of the Fleet Marine Force could not be temporized with. The retention and continuation of the separate identity of the Navy was an absolute in any postwar national security reorganization. The most satisfactory solution was the Eberstadt Plan. If, however, there had to be a single civilian secretary then the problem became one of so defining his authority that the same goal was achieved.

Forrestal's reluctance to confront the issue of a Secretary of Defense can be seen in his original conception of the role of the secretary. He would be a point for ultimate decision on only the most fundamental questions. The authority of the secretary must be stated in such terms that the separate services and their secretaries would be free to establish their policies. It was imperative to establish only a most "general authority" for the secretary in order to preclude his accomplishing through directive what the Navy would not permit through legislation. The vital issue of roles and missions for the services must be clearly outside the jurisdiction of the secretary. While the authority of the secretary would be general, Forrestal insisted on a detailed language that would make merger by fiat impossible. Acceptance in principle and acceptance of certain crucial details must go hand in hand in this instance. The loose federalism envisaged by Eberstadt is now presided over by a single civilian secretary as well as by the proposed boards with the interrelationships only vaguely defined.

The early thinking of Secretary Forrestal is summarized in a letter from Ferdinand Eberstadt to John J. McCloy which grew out of discussions at Brown Brothers, Harriman & Company in New York:

> . . . the Secretary of National Defense shall coordinate various matters of common or conflicting interest between the three military departments; final decision on these questions were subject to the President's decision . . . the Secretary of National Defense would have authority to integrate the budget, coordinate and integrate logistic and procurement matters, research programs . . . general power to determine conflict between the services, use and development of weapons where they are in dispute; and also generally to settle conflicts and disputes between military departments . . . This Department and Secretary shall have no general or specific responsibility with respect to the administration of the three military departments, nor any general control over them other than authority specifically conferred upon him, nor any right to interfere within.[9]

Having received the counsel of the "Brown Brothers, Harriman Group," Forrestal asked Admiral Forrest P.

Sherman to evaluate from the standpoint of the Navy a paper developed outside of that service. Sherman crystallized the irreducible position on roles and missions: any definition of functions of the services must provide for "the continuance of the Marine Corps and . . . safeguard naval aviation including anti-submarine warfare and naval reconnaissance components."[10]

The Assistant Secretary of War for Air, Stuart Symington, in sharp contrast to his predecessor, Lovett, emerged as the major antagonist for Forrestal. (Lovett, indeed, had participated in the Brown Brothers, Harriman development of the Navy position.) Symington was spokesman for the autonomous organization of air power and, consequently, found himself at loggerheads with the Navy. By January 1947, Secretary of War Robert A. Patterson felt constrained to tell Forrestal of his concern over "growing evidence of bitterness between the services." For his part Forrestal could only reply that the project for a single department would not be successful "unless the two services were honestly and throughly back of a plan";[11] there was the suggestion that Symington was departing from agreed-upon ground. At the same time, Forrestal was arraying himself against the position taken by President Truman, who was still disposed to accept Army thinking on a single department. Truman was interested in what he chose to call "real unification," either immediately or, if that were not possible, over the long term.[12] This carried him well past the last Navy redoubt. The "new viewpoints, new doctrines, and new habits of thinking" which Truman called for in presenting the 1947 National Security Bill to Congress were by no means self-evidently valid in the judgment of the Secretary of the Navy: indeed, they constituted a rejection of much hard experience which he felt dictated the principal elements of his own plan.

Forrestal went before the Congress in the first half of 1947 with the conviction that he was already supporting a compromise measure, that he had already compromised his own basic views in the matter. Forrestal had abandoned his early opposition to a single department and a single secretary and had worked reluctantly toward the definition of the secretary's authority. As a result, the bill now before Congress was designed to accommodate diverse interests. "If any single item were withdrawn or modified to the advantage of any one service," Forrestal argued with some urgency, "the mutual accomodation would be thrown out of balance."[13] Then, speaking directly to the matter of the authority of the Secretary of National Defense, he stressed that the secretary would "exercise overall direction but will not go down into the departments themselves and deal with their functions, daily operations and administration." Forrestal added rather curtly, "my support for the bill is based on that expectation."[14] Ries sums up with a point that clearly was Forrestal's as well: "How the system would operate depended as much upon the way the secretary of defense sought to use his authority, and how he viewed his role, as upon the various provisions of the law."[15] The Secretary of National Defense on the basis of a general authority would have power at the apex of the department to make overall policy decisions guaranteeing the link between policy and operations. He would not be a "manager" who would "interfere" in the operational preserve of the services. This difficult relationship between the apex and the service level would hinge more on the men who held the key positions than on functions and authority elaborately defined in a statute. The Secretary of National Defense, it followed, must have the right to select his own assistants who, to be sure, would be few in number. Above all it would matter who the Secretary of National Defense was.

James V. Forrestal became the first man to preside over the entire military establishment of the United States because he had through a painful and protracted period found common ground with Harry Truman. That the Secretary of the Navy brought the President to an understanding and acceptance of his most basic convictions, and that the President had no reservations in making this appointment, is a measure of both men.[16] Writing to William C. Potter shortly after assuming his new office, Secretary Forrestal reflected on the struggle of the previous two years: "My chief misgivings about unification derived from my fear that there would be a tendency toward over concentration and reliance on one man or one group direction. In other words too much central control—which I know you will agree, is one of the troubles with the world today. A lot of admittedly brainy men believe that governments, history, science and business can be rationalized into a state of perfection."[17] Undoubtedly, it would be incorrect to suggest that Forrestal assumed his new duties with any sense of foreboding. It is more accurate to describe his outlook as one of somber realism. In any event, it is important to note the impact of a short tenure in office on his conception of the role of the secretary. There was determination from the outset that the concept he had fought so arduously for could be proven out in practice—the consequences of failure could only be disasterous. The specter of overconcentration could be dealt with by the dispersion of the policy-making process to all levels and all services. As secretary, he would transmit the guidelines of the administration to all components of the department and, in turn, would oversee the policy-formulation process. Executive authority and direction over operations would be decentralized; the Secretary of National Defense would be useful in this realm largely in the sense of removing friction between component parts. Forrestal would rely on his men: "he had a deep and discerning distrust of dictation in any form, even his own, and his constant impulse was to understand and adjust rather than to rush to conclusions and issue orders."[18] The apex would be a "clearinghouse," keeping lines open to all elements of the structure for information and ideas, ultimately determining what policies best implemented national guidelines.

Forrestal was immediately confronted with a major test of his role concept in the preparation of the fiscal year 1949 budget. In the interval between World War II and the Korean War, the President was prepared to entertain only the most stringent defense budgets, and in this respect at least the Congress was disposed to cooperation. The services, moreover, understood fully that the first budget "go-round" under the new organization would be critical from the standpoint of relative status, and as a result the unification battle was again opened up. The Secretary of Defense's initial assessment of the matter showed him adhering strictly to his prescribed role. The policy implications of the administration's budget estimates were his first concern. Forrestal was acutely aware, perhaps more so than anyone else in Washington at this time, that a "Cold War" was underway with a former ally, the Soviet Union. Given his understanding that policy was the prime element in the responsibility of the Secretary of Defense, Forrestal felt compelled to convey his own sense of alarm both within the government and, as far as possible, to the public. At the same time he was prepared as a member of the Cabinet to publicly defend the positions taken by the President.

The service secretaries were directed to make all efforts to bring their estimates within the guidelines set by the administration. The dilemma was not lost upon the secretary: how could the public be made aware of the grave implications of the Cold War when the administration was bent on maintaining reduced defense budgets? Such concerns were the privilege of elevated office; they were not in evidence at the service level. Symington was not hesitant to propose that in view of the "primacy" of strategic air power the largest share of the defense budget should be allocated to the Air Force. He made it quite clear that he was not bound by a "Navy Concept" of the Air Force's mission and introduced his own 70-Group plan. Basing his remarks on a statement from the Joint Chiefs of Staff, Forrestal responded to the 70-Group proposal that while he supported an overall increase in force levels, this must reflect a "balanced increase" in strength. He told the House Armed Services Committee, "I think it is very

dangerous to select any part of our national military power
without being sure that elements necessary to go with it are
present in sufficient power and force to make it usable . . . you cannot separate in modern war one segment
from the other . . . they march together." [19] The Joint Chiefs
of Staff, however, had not been specific about the allocation
of increases for each service, leaving the matter in the hands
of the Secretary of National Defense. Now a subordinate was
offering testimony, threatening not only the balanced-force
idea but Forrestal's very concept of the office of secretary.
Needless to say, there had been no provision in this concept
for a "rebellion" by one of the services; and it had not been
anticipated that one of the subordinates might well have
more influence externally than the secretary.

Forrestal was realistic enough to appreciate that an unforeseen situation had, in fact, come to pass. Outside support
for the Air Force dictated that he compromise his views;
whether the secretary was caught short as a result of the JCS
posture on the budget is another matter, however. Warren R.
Schilling, in his study of the 1950 budget, stresses a lack of
realism about the role of the Joint Chiefs in the policy process on Forrestal's part, an analysis in which Ries concurs.
But if one keeps in view Forrestal's reasons for maintaining
the JCS as representative of the separate services, it is difficult to conclude that he was naive in his expectations about
what could be accomplished by them in the way of "policy."
The factor of a rising concurrence between Truman and
Symington on both political and military grounds needs more
emphasis. Paul Y. Hammond suggests that Forrestal somehow
had a clearer view of British executive authority than the
American presidential system. Again, there is little reason to
believe that Forrestal was unaware of the autonomous and
"final" authority of the President. Conflict arose between
Mr. Truman and the Secretary of Defense because Forrestal
did not choose to give up an independent policy role of his
own in favor of an "administrative" role as did Secretaries

Louis Johnson, Wilson, and McElroy.[20] There appears to be no dispute over the fact that Secretary Forrestal recognized the need for greater authority to realize his own conception of the office. It would be necessary on the basis of experience to ask for a new deal of the cards. In the first annual report of the Secretary of Defense,[21] James V. Forrestal revised his views somewhat about what is required to guarantee that the secretary not have "the dummy hand." Integration of policy at the apex remains the primary responsibility of the secretary; however, it is now evident that in order to accomplish this, "direction, authority and control" over the department and agencies of the national military establishment must be vested in the secretary. Significantly, Forrestal proposes that the key word in the 1947 act defining the authority of the secretary—"general"—be stricken. Unsatisfied with the ability of the Joint Chiefs to come to policy conclusions, he proposes that they have a chairman. In spite of the fact that the crisis of the first year turned around budgetary allocations and in spite of the fact that Forrestal desired nothing more than a real relationship between strategy and money, he did not join with the Hoover Commission in proposing a comptroller at the "Defense" level. [22] The "clearinghouse" function of the secretary was not tied up with budgetary control from the apex, as important as tight budgets were in Forrestal's brief term. Yet another recommendation would suffice in this respect; namely, that the three services would lose their Cabinet status and become military departments within the Department of Defense. This should preclude any recurrence of the events of the previous year. Forrestal saw these recommendations as "practical measures," stemming from working experience, which were necessary to give reality to a role concept which in its essential spirit remained unchanged.

Robert A. Lovett

In the admiring phrase of Senator Henry M. Jackson,

"perhaps more than any other living American he [Robert A. Lovett] is 'Mr. National Security.' "[23] A colleague, friend, and disciple of James V. Forrestal, Lovett was a ranking figure in the "Cold War Cadre." Huntington describes this cadre, the "Truman men," in admiring terms. They

> ... tended to be the investment banker type, concerned less with the concrete production of things and more with the subtle intricacies of high finance ... the background of these bankers and lawyers gave them a perspective on affairs quite different from that of the usual American industrialist ... they possessed all the inherent and real conservatism of the banking breed. Transferred to government, they were cautious realists, aware of the complexities of human affairs, the limitations of human foresight and control, and the dangers of extending commitments beyond resources. They were also in some measure another manifestation of the curious way in which Theodore Roosevelt was the intellectual godfather of Democratic administrations after 1933. Former progressives such as Ickes had contributed much to the New Deal. A clear line existed from Root to Stimson to Marshall, Lovett and McCloy. After the war the influence of the Forrestal men who spread throughout the government contributed a similar perspective to national policy.[24]

Lovett's career reads as if it were the contrivance of a script writer (it has been summarized by Lovett himself with the phrase "I was lucky"): born in Texas before the turn of the century; winner of the Navy Cross in World War I; educated at Yale and Harvard; after five years partner in Brown Brothers, Harriman & Company; Assistant Secretary of War for Air; Under Secretary of State; Deputy Secretary of Defense; Secretary of Defense; member of the President's Board of Consultants on Foreign Intelligence Activities; advisor to administrations officially and unofficially for a quarter of a century. Lovett understood the objectives of Forrestal as few men did and personally sought to bring them to realization. His own experience in the national security apparatus, most particularly as Secretary of Defense, gives his conceptualization of the role of the secretary unquestioned significance. The twin pillars of an "objectivist" conceptualization, the primacy of policy and the integrity of professionalism, are the essential characteristics of Lovett's understanding; this understanding issues in a generalist role for the Secretary of Defense that is an extension of the position of Forrestal. [25]

Serving as deputy to General George C. Marshall, both in the Department of State and thereafter in the Department of Defense, Lovett put a premium on "constant, close and sympathetic cooperation" between the two departments. And, he added, "the tone of the cooperation must be set by the secretaries." The fate of his predecessor at the Pentagon, Louis Johnson, was clearly in his mind. "Perfectly legitimate and, occasionally, valuable" differences of opinion at the policy level would arise between State and Defense. But a court of domestic and foreign relations, with the President presiding, before which the "vigorous staffs" of the two departments could put views, would make the final formulation of policy. This is the process of the "prior step" which is required for effective military policy and strategic planning. In emphasizing its necessity, Lovett harks back to the "leading spirit," Forrestal, who, he said, attempted to get "this form of court, in effect, over which the President would preside, so that you could get a decision in the light of all the facts." [26] The decision could only be that of the President, but it must come as the result of hard staff work by the departments operationally concerned addressing themselves to clearly defined issues. No question of the paramount role of the Department of State in external affairs is raised by the former under secretary; rather it is underlined by him. The Department of Defense through the secretary is a contributor to national policy guidelines in those areas of operational concern. The real problem in this area is succinctly put by Secretary of Defense Marshall in his instructions to Deputy Secretary Lovett: "Comprise long-standing policy differences between Defense and State, and . . . mesh operations of the two together so that political commitments have armed strength to back them up." [27]

In arguing the primacy of policy, Lovett underlines the importance of civilian determination of national objectives and at the same time takes account of a cardinal tenet of military professionalism. In order to be most effective, the military has consistently argued that they must have clear guidelines within which to plan and conduct operations. The point has been stated felicitously by General Maxwell Taylor: the military must "be sure that the sword forged by the Armed Forces is the one which the civilian leadership wants placed in its hands."[28] It is the overriding responsibility of the Secretary of Defense to take part in the formulation of national policy and in turn to guarantee that the military posture that is called for is forged. In the formulation of national security policy, the secretary will rely upon and will require contributions from the military professionals in Lovett's view. But the military are not "makers of national political policies. They are trained to carry out such policy, not to originate it. They clearly cannot do their planning job until a higher level fixes national goals."[29] A prominent example of Lovett's point was his effective working relationships with the Air Chiefs (Hoyt S. Vandenberg, Nathan F. Twining, Curtis E. LeMay) in the development of the B-52 program.

Distinguishing further the roles of the secretary and the civilian leadership of the Department of Defense on the one hand, and of the Joint Chiefs of Staff on the other, in the realm of policy, Lovett told the Jackson Subcommittee: "Civilian and military executives alike should stick to the fields in which they have special training and aptitudes: if they do, the chance of making the machinery work is excellent. One of the few humans as exasperating as a civilian businessman who suddenly becomes an expert on military strategy and tactics is the military adviser who magically becomes an expert on some highly sophisticated production problem in which he has no background of experience."[30] He argued that split papers from the Joint Chiefs were not inherently objectionable: "it is vitally important to a Secretary of Defense, as one of the advisors of the President, with a special responsibility, to know what the alternatives are to a course of action, or what serious obstacles to a proposed program are foreseen by a responsible Chief of Staff." [31] Lovett would not countenance any restructuring of the Joint Chiefs of Staff which would break the "close relationship between planning and operational responsibility." The best professional results can be anticipated from the military when those responsible for strategic planning have at the same time overall operational responsibility. While a link must be maintained on professional grounds, it would be opposed to professional integrity to tie military and political factors together through special career programs for selected officers. Such a "fusionist" idea was the antithesis of all objectivist-realist thought among both civilians and military.

As Deputy Secretary of Defense, Lovett worked under the nation's first soldier. Not unexpectedly General Marshall adhered to procedures which had proved themselves in his long military career. The recommendation of the Hoover Commission that "The Secretary of Defense be relieved, as far as possible, of the burden of routine administration" struck a responsive chord. Marshall made it clear at the outset that the deputy secretary's authority was such that it "exercises command over the Secretaries of War, Air, and Navy." [32] At the same time assistant secretaries would play a major administrative role in preparing and systematizing the flow of information to the clearinghouse at the apex. Marshall did not propose to be active in a policy role; he intended rather to clear proposals for the most part from the Joint Chiefs with whom he was basically attuned. The deputy secretary could not be in sympathy intellectually with the role Marshall set for himself. Lovett was not prepared to let the initiative and the machinery for policy take up location elsewhere. The complex question of how the policy role becomes operational for the Secretary of Defense—that is, the question of his working relationship with the JCS, the assistant secretaries, and the service secretaries as well as his relationships with his own staff—has been the subject of considerable discussion, much of it with reference to the tenure of Secretary Lovett. Some expansion of the more general points already made about Lovett's role concept, therefore, is required.

The framework within which strategic doctrine and strategic planning can evolve effectively and meaningfully consists of criteria which, taken together, may be designated as national security policy. The latter is the fundamental responsibility of civilian authority, the former of military professionalism. Needless to say, a clear-cut relationship between the Secretary of Defense and the Joint Chiefs of Staff embodying this dichotomy is, for all practical purposes, difficult to achieve. What is important, however, is that the distinction be recognized and efforts be directed toward its realization. If the maxim holds that "it is the man who makes the office," then certainly the need for policy assistance may be met by different secretaries in different ways. It is not set in granite, for example, that a Secretary of Defense cannot obtain policy assistance from those with operational responsibilities in the department. In his relationships with the JCS, Lovett insisted on the policy prerogatives of the civilian side subject to "advice" from the military. He was disposed to consider policy questions directly with the service secretaries and with his own assistant secretaries. It has been contended that in doing so "he sought to place major decisions, such as force levels and budgets, with . . subordinates he could more easily control," and that this constituted an "undermining" and a "bypass" of the Joint Chiefs of Staff. [33] There is enough in the writings, speeches, and testimony of Secretary Lovett to disregard any contention that he sought to put major policy decisions outside his own purview. Indeed, his suggestion that the Secretary of Defense become, in effect, the Deputy Commander in Chief is probably the strongest recommendation ever made in behalf of a policy role for the secretary.[34]

Huntington has put the point about staff for the Secretary of Defense well when he writes that "the important issue [is] not how much staff the Secretary [has], but rather what kind of staff . . . a staff is only a real aid to an executive when its outlook is his outlook and its interest is his interest."[35] Aid is where you find it. If the basic rationale for Secretary of Defense staff is policy assistance, then that assistance will be obtained from men with a policy perspective. A table of organization is not necessarily helpful in this respect. Lovett did expect that the comptroller would look at JCS recommendations in the light of fiscal criteria, undeniably an aspect of civilian policy responsibility. But no doubt the significant point here is that the Secretary of Defense is Robert A. Lovett and the Comptroller is Wilfred J. McNeil. If the principle that unites strategic planning responsibility and operational responsibility in the JCS is sound, it may be a useful principle on the civilian side. Huntington's strictures against the enhanced role of the comptroller after 1953 arise precisely because the Lovett concept of policy supremacy as the definition of civilian supremacy is no longer in force.

What Lovett's actions seem to suggest most of all is not a special civilian-military staff, which he considered at one point, but no special staff as such. The suggestion is more of informal arrangements among "special men" committed to the supremacy of policy. Unanimity will not be the result of such arrangements; however, it would be idle to suggest that this is what is being sought. At bottom Lovett rejected panaceas for efficiency and streamlining; it was "wholly unrealistic to talk of making government simple." With Forrestal he saw a degree of "organized disorder" as a virtue. He reminded the Jackson Subcommittee of the "often forgotten fact" that "our form of Government, and its machinery, has had built into it a series of clashes of groups . . . this device in inviting argument between conflicting interests was obviously the result of a decision to give up the doubtful efficiency of one group control."[36] If there were a point to organization and management, it was to thrive on the disorder of conflicting interests and distinct professional competences, and to distill from them a rare blend. The Secretary of Defense had the enormously difficult role of the generalist.

Thomas S. Gates

The Forrestal-Lovett articulation of the role of the Secretary of Defense is submerged in 1953 and does not again find embodiment until Thomas S. Gates—cut to the Forrestal-Lovett lines—becomes Secretary of Defense in 1959. [37] The Gates tenure in office of little more than one year is the concluding stage in the conceptualization of the objectivist-realist understanding. This understanding is significant beyond its term, however. Following the 1953 and 1958 Reorganization Acts, a steady trend of centralization in the Department of Defense, and the tenures of two men wholly outside the generalist schema, Gates demonstrated that events had not made the Forrestal-Lovett understanding anachronistic. What is at issue ultimately is an understanding, an outlook, an appraisal of men and their institutions. Thomas S. Gates, to a remarkable degree kith and kin with the "Truman men," brought their understanding to bear on the office of the Secretary of Defense at the onset of the 1960s.

A lifelong Philadelphian (born April 10, 1906), Gates joined Drexel and Company in 1928 after his graduation from the University of Pennsylvania. He was made a partner in 1940 but thereupon served three years in the Navy during World War II, rising to the rank of Captain. With the advent of the Eisenhower administration, he began his government career as Under Secretary of the Navy in October 1953. In April 1957 he became Secretary of the Navy, serving until February 1959. Four months later, on the death of the

Thomas S. Gates 41

Deputy Secretary of Defense, Donald A. Quarles, Mr. Gates assumed that office with the informal stipulation that he would succeed to the office of Secretary of Defense upon the retirement of Mr. Neil McElroy. He became Secretary of Defense on December 2, 1959, serving to the end of Mr. Eisenhower's second term on January 20, 1961. The parallels not only of background but of experience between Gates and his intellectual precursors, Forrestal and Lovett, were not lost on the Jackson Subcommittee during its inquiry into national policy machinery in 1960-61. Joining with Senator John A. Stennis, Jackson attributed the "highly satisfactory" relationship between Gates and the Joint Chiefs of Staff to "his previous experience over a period of years within the Department of Defense. You cannot deal with professional soldiers and make decisions," Jackson emphasized, "unless you have had that experience."[38] Outside the scope of Jackson's inquiry was the role concept Gates brought to the office and further refined during his term. Gates, however, made this manifestly clear. A primary concern with policy and a professional regard for the military marked him even in the context of the post-1958 Department of Defense as a Forrestal-Lovett man.

Gates found the working relationships between Defense and State "excellent" and staunchly defended the National Security Council procedures for the determination of national policy guidelines. Echoing the views of Lovett, he underscored the validity of overall national policy coming to a head in the National Security Council as a result of staff work done in the departments concerned. In response to the suggestion of Professor Walt W. Rostow that the National Security Council "would be vastly improved if it had an independent staff of first-rate men, freed of ties to particular bureaucracies, paid to think in terms of the totality of our policy problems, empowered to lay proposals on the table," Gates remarked abruptly: "This is an ivory tower staff created out of first-rate men free, apparently, of all experience and association with the problems." [39] (A decade later it is not clear whether Professor Rostow would not agree with Secretary Gates.) Concerned about the policy role of the Joint Chiefs of Staff during the terms of his two immediate predecessors, Gates sought to reestablish relationships between the secretary and the JCS which would maximize strategic factors in the development of policy. In his first appearance before the Subcommittee on Defense Appropriations of the House Appropriations Committee, the new Secretary of Defense spoke with some feeling on the issue:

> I believe in the Joint Chiefs of Staff. I believe it is a system that has been successful in two wars. I am not afraid of divided opinions. I believe they are healthy. I think the problem arises on how decisions are made as a result of those divided opinions . . . If civilian control is to be meaningful—and it is meaningful because the President is Commander-in-Chief—then civilians must take the responsibility for making the decisions, and they can only do this on an informed basis. An informed basis to me means working closely with the Joint Chiefs of Staff so that the civilians can be educated and propertly informed. They should not exclude themselves on the basis that they are not wise enough to make military decisions. I intend to work that way and I hope it will prove to be constructive. I do not subscribe to the "cure-alls" that are suggested such as a single Chief of Staff. I do not know what good that does. That ends up in a single opinion. We do not always want a single opinion. [40]

Less than a month after his appointment, Gates told the JCS he would sit with them when it was necessary to resolve divisions of opinion. The Gates directive of December 29, 1959, looked to the prompt and expeditious resolution of disputes when they arose. [41] This step on the part of Secretary Gates was to bring the Joint Chiefs into the realm of policy and budget discussions to a degree that had not as yet obtained in the Eisenhower administration. Gates presented a detailed statement of his views on the role of the Secretary of Defense and his relations with the Joint Chiefs to the Special Preparedness Subcommittee of the Senate Committee on

Armed Services in January 1962. He said, in part, that the secretary "can accept, change, or disagree completely with his planners. If his position is at variance with that of the Secretary of State, the question will go to the President for decision . . . at the time of decision, the role of the military ceases. Their contribution is never ending as advisors and planners, and their opinions are important and should be heard. They may influence policy, but decision is not theirs and they ought not create policy." This is perhaps the most succinct statement of the generalist viewpoint. Concurring with Secretary Lovett that "split papers" were not objectionable, Gates told the Jackson Subcommittee: "We are dealing with matters of judgment. We are considering matters of great complexity. Senior military men of integrity do not compromise their views when they think our national security is at stake. They will have differences of opinion, and it is natural and helpful to have them." [42] Nonetheless, decisions would have to be made, made by civilians.

Obviously satisfied with the steps Gates had taken, the Jackson Subcommittee pressed him further on a related matter. Senator Stennis was particularly concerned about a high-level policy staff of military men still linked to their respective services: "I am increasingly convinced that it is just frightful to have policy decisions, even though the men are able and highly patriotic, made by military personnel that are still responsible to one particular service for their promotions and for their future." Gates had no enthusiasm for what might well be a "decisive change" in the concept of the Joint Chiefs of Staff system: "we are getting good results from the present system in the policy level. Most of the problems that I think worry you, worry me and are not at that level. They are at lower levels in the services . . . I would not undermine it [the JCS system] or change it, unless I was awfully sure that another type of system would really be an improvement. I am not convinced that it would be." [43] As part of the career planning for selected officers, Gates ordered Joint Staff assignments with the Unified Commands and with international commands to implement the direct-line arrangement between the Joint Chiefs and the Unified Commands. But again Gates made it clear that the purpose of such an order was not to establish "super-staffs," or to put rank and promotion outside the control of the officer's service. "It may be that someone will be foolish enough to permit super-staffs to develop at the expense of combat officers," the secretary remarked, but he would not countenance it.[44] Gates had saved the bedrock principle of the Joint Chiefs of Staff system as it had developed out of World War II and had been reconfirmed in the National Security Acts of 1947 and 1949. The chiefs would maintain the "vital link" between strategic planning and operational responsibility. They would do this as a plural entity. Throughout the 1960s the case for a single chief of staff, and for a military council divorced from the services, would not be pressed; Gates' direct and intimate experience in the interstices of the Pentagon was a decisive factor.

Gates was persuaded that the Secretary of Defense had ample authority before the 1958 Reorganization Act: "I have believed most of my time in Washington that the Secretary of Defense had a great deal of authority. I thought he had a great deal of authority when Secretary Johnson cancelled an aircraft carrier before I ever came down here. I thought Mr. Wilson had the authority to do almost anything he wanted to do by ordering me to do it when I was in the U.S. Navy Department . . . if there was any question about authority before, there is no question about it now."[45] With more authority than either Forrestal or Lovett possessed, or perhaps wanted, Gates nonetheless underscored his concurrence in the concept of a generalist role for the Secretary of Defense. In words that sounded as if they must have come from James Forrestal, Gates stated a basic belief: "I have been one who believed that you must in the most modern sense decentralize and hold people responsible, and then coordinate.

The British seem to be great coordinators. I don't know whether this is true or not. *But coordination in its true sense is a very difficult art for an American because he wants to run something.*" [46] The Secretary of Defense who eschewed coordination of a decentralized, pluralist, professional system, preferring instead to run or manage the system as chief functional participant, was the antithesis of the Forrestal-Lovett-Gates thesis.

The enhanced status of the Joint Chiefs of Staff confirms the effort of the secretary to implement his role concept. Also striking is his refusal to utilize the budgetary process as a device for centralizing power in the office of the Secretary of Defense: "a particular effort was made to assure that all the principal officials of the Department of Defense—the Service Secretaries, the Assistant Secretaries of Defense, and the Chiefs of Staff, both in their individual capacities and in their corporate capacity as the Joint Chiefs of Staff—participated in the review of the annual program and budget." [47] Gates candidly indicated that neither he, as Secretary of the Navy, nor the Joint Chiefs of Staff had participated in the budget process in this manner in the past. Now all parties concerned would have the same data and analyses available to them that the secretary would have and at the same time. The comptroller was not utilized in any policy sense such as were the Joint Chiefs. Gates did find the newly established Director of Defense Research and Engineering helpful on the formulation of the budget but, again, as a coordinator or clearinghouse agent in weapons development. In this area especially, "flexibility" in the budget was a desideratum given the pace of technological change. It was inflexibility that caused Gates to reject the "functional" budget: to put the budget on a functional basis was "extremely difficult to do because a lot of our systems do not fall into a functional area . . . It is almost impossible to do with a multipurpose system, like an aircraft carrier, for example . . . flexibility in the budget is helpful, and accountability, I think, could be made to go with it in some way that might ease the rigidity of an annual review." [48] Thomas S. Gates turned over the office of the Secretary of Defense to Robert S. McNamara in January 1961, having reaffirmed the vitality of a generalist role. Mr. McNamara, however, would not choose to follow the course set by the "Truman men."

The Eisenhower-Rockefeller Schema: Charles E. Wilson

A distinct and opposed concept of the role of the Secretary of Defense, his position in the national security apparatus, and the interrelationships between the secretary and the Joint Chiefs of Staff is a major by-product of the Eisenhower years. It should not be surprising that General of the Army Dwight D. Eisenhower, President of the United States from 1953 to 1961, was the most influential factor in the determination of this concept. The impact of President Eisenhower's views on national security policy and on the roles of the Secretary of Defense and the Joint Chiefs, by and large, has been underestimated. The President was firm and insistent in his establishment of the basic guidelines of national security policy and how the national security apparatus should function. He personally considered and then made the major strategic decisions; he selected the major weapon systems; he outlined the organizational reforms brought about in the Department of Defense. As Mr. Eisenhower put it himself, "my military background assured at least that as President I would hold certain definite convictions on national security." [49] In the endeavor of taking a "new look" at the Department of Defense, Eisenhower had as a "principal advisor" Nelson A. Rockefeller of New York. Rockefeller was unusually active as a consultant on Defense Department organization and a powerful contributor to a conception of the secretary's role that is quite at odds with the Forrestal-Lovett-Gates formulation. Chairman of the President's Advisory Committee on

Government Organization from 1953 to 1958, Rockefeller headed the 1953 Committee on Department of Defense Organization and in 1958 was appointed consultant to the Committee on the Organization of the Department of Defense. In 1960 Rockefeller put before the Jackson Subcommittee on National Policy Machinery a complete statement of what we shall call a functionalist role concept of the Secretary of Defense.

The Eisenhower-Rockefeller concept was functionalist, first and foremost, in its sharp demarcation of policy and administration. Not only would the President of the United States have ultimate responsibility for national security policy, he would be the architect and prime mover. The imposing credentials of the President in the realm of national security made him the unquestioned center of the policy process. Eisenhower, in the aftermath of the Korean War, had accepted the military postulate that "the best means of achieving military security is through the maintenance of substantial forces in being." This was a fact of life in the Cold War; still, the President was determined that through personal control of "policy," largely through the device of budgets that avoided "peaks and valleys" and reflected the economic and fiscal state of the nation, the concept of civilian control could still be meaningful. [50] On the other hand, the Secretary of Defense must have the fullest authority to effectively perform his function, namely, the efficient implementation of presidential policy directives. The President would make every effort to provide the secretary with the necessary authority.

The special Committee on Department of Defense Organization, under Mr. Rockefeller, took cognizance of the President's functional distinction between policy and administration in a study directed particularly to "the position of the Secretary of Defense."[51] The secretary would not be a focal point of policy; rather he was envisaged as a "management specialist" who would resolve administrative problems.

Particular attention was directed to the assistant secretary level and a question which would vex the department for a number of years. It was agreed that the "outside boards and agencies," basic to the Forrestal-Eberstadt administrative concept, would be abolished and that their "functions" would be brought within the purview of assistant secretaries. This raised a formidable issue: would the assistant secretaries thereby become managers in their respective functional areas with "command" over the service secretaries, or would they simply constitute additional "staff" assistance for the Secretary of Defense who, alone, would "manage" the department? The position of the committee in the spring of 1953 was clear enough. The assistant secretaries would be "just exactly what they were intended to be—top level staff assistants to the Secretary of Defense"; above all, they would not "give orders to the Service Secretaries."[52] What occurred in the Department of Defense between 1953 and 1958 ran contrary to the stated views of the committee but, undoubtedly, not to the private views of the President who would undertake to render into law in 1958 the de facto practices of the preceding five years.

So long as the Secretary of Defense was seen as the chief management functionary in the department with supervision and control over each operational area, the assistant secretaries, posted at each major point of contact with the services, found that "supervision and control" in their individual areas had a somewhat abstract quality unless they, too, exercised the management authority of their chief. The important issue, however, is not the inevitable rise of the command authority of the assistant secretaries, but the conception of the role of the Secretary of Defense that is involved. Professor Hammond (to whom the author is indebted for his analysis of the Eisenhower period) observes that "the continual increase in the number of functional controls held and the amount of actual operating performed in OSD [was] out of all proportion to the small increase in the systematic making by the Secretary of Defense of general policy . . . as a consequence, OSD has tended to be confined to a management outlook in the supervision of the military establishment."[53] What Hammond does not underscore is that this did not occur willy-nilly but was precisely the development of a role concept of the Secretary of Defense that Mr. Eisenhower sought to put into operation.

At the suggestion of General Lucius Clay, an indisputably successful management team from General Motors, Charles E. Wilson and Roger Kyes, took over the helm of the Department of Defense. A powerful, flamboyant personality, "Engine Charlie" Wilson was bound to make his predecessors seem bland. Ideally suited to the Eisenhower concept, Wilson was prepared to "leave the military stuff up to the military" and take charge of what he called "production"; he would "manage" not "make" military policy.[54] Consistent with the division of labor which left the JCS chairman, Admiral Arthur W. Radford, if not the other chiefs, responsible for military policy advice to the President and the National Security Council, Wilson set about to put the department on a businesslike basis. Deputy Secretary Kyes and Comptroller Wilfred J. McNeil (continuing in a new milieu) had responsibility for the budget. In keeping with Rockefeller Committee recommendations, "Vice-Presidents" took over the old Munitions Board and the Research and Development Board. An Assistant Secretary of Defense (the able Donald Quarles) now headed up an Office of Research and Development, and another Assistant Secretary of Defense (chainstore executive Charles B. Thomas) had charge of an Office of Supply and Logistics. H. Struve Hensel, like Thomas an "old Forrestal man," was appointed to the new post of General Counsel. It was Thomas' initial task to put a new worth on the entire national military establishment. At the same time Comptroller McNeil introduced the "Stock-Fund" and "Industrial Fund" devices for management control over Department of Defense inventories. Such "efficiency measures" had as their singular purpose the administrative implementation of the policy line provided directly by the President and were in accord with reorganization proposals from Mr. Rockefeller.

While Wilson, on the whole, was content to stand aside from the process of policy formulation and concentrate on the achievement of efficiency and savings, he found the President's "new look" guidelines difficult in the execution at times. Mr. Eisenhower's order to cut military manpower 10 percent in January 1955 seemed designed to aggravate relations with Army Chief of Staff General Matthew B. Ridgway. Wilson was not anxious to have a repeat of the embroglio with General Hoyt S. Vandenberg who had recommended the Lovett projections on the Air Force before being relieved. Such conflicts were unavoidable for a man who did not pretend to understand the military much less the institution of the Joint Chiefs of Staff. He confided to his successor, Neil H. McElroy, that "with a few exceptions in the higher ranks, it was pretty hard to get those fellows to think about defense programs in terms of the aggregate national problem, as distinct from the interests of their services."[55] Brilliantly reflecting the "fusionist" theme of Mr. Eisenhower and Mr. Rockefeller, Wilson believed that just as the civilian leadership should focus on "the aggregate national problem," so should the military. There was little recognition of the unique professional task of the JCS to contribute "a military point of view" to the policy process. Indeed, the Joint Chiefs were directed by Wilson to "avail themselves of the most competent and considered thinking" outside the military realm as a basis for their judgments. In any event, the JCS, while under the authority of the secretary, were outside his span of concern; they would have to resolve their disputes ultimately with the President. Wilson rejected the coordinator role as outside his functional specialty.

Still, the secretary apparently felt compelled to maintain the closest possible contact with the President, with whom he was more at ease. Sherman Adams writes: "In his stormy term as Secretary of Defense, Wilson had leaned upon Eisenhower with his intimate knowledge of the defense establishment and its personalities a little more than the President wanted anybody in his Cabinet to lean upon him. Wilson wanted an hour a week alone with Eisenhower to discuss routine problems many of which the President thought Wilson should solve himself . . . Wilson complained later that he did not see the President often enough to obtain necessary guidance but the President did not have any such concern." Actually, Wilson had few qualms or suggestions about the role of the Secretary of Defense. For his own part he thought he might ultimately be more interested in research and development matters than "what might be called organization and operations."[56]

The Joint Chiefs of Staff were at the center of Mr. Eisenhower's concerns from the very outset. To begin with, he sharply distinguished the roles of the JCS and the Secretary of Defense, adding another dimension to his functionalism. The President assumed that the major policy contributions from the Department of Defense would come from the Joint Chiefs of Staff, in most instances through the chairman. As General Robert Cutler has put it, the President expected "the Chairman of the Joint Chiefs of Staff to represent the Chiefs at the [National Security Council] table, and the Secretary to represent the service secretaries."[57] The Secretary of Defense, Mr. Eisenhower has written, was to be "my channel for communicating decisions to the defense establishment."[58] In the elaboration and development of national security policy, some interplay between the President and the Chiefs would take place; these discussions would not call for any major participation on the part of the management specialist. It would be necessary, however, if the policy discussions were to be effective, for the Chiefs to have a thorough understanding of all the environmental factors which impinge on "military policy." The first step would be the selection of new Chiefs of Staff and, above all, a new chairman.

The President had sought to strengthen the position of

the chairman and the Joint Staff in the 1953 Reorganization
Act after having identified the man who would become chairman of the Joint Chiefs. "My objective," writes the President, "was to take at least one step in divorcing the thinking
and the outlook of the members of the Joint Staff from
those of the parent services and to center their entire effort
on national planning for the overall common defense." [59]
The Congress, not prepared to make the Joint Staff simply
the vehicle of the chairman, did provide for its enlargement.
The President wanted a new outlook among his Chiefs which
would amount to a sharing in and wholehearted cooperation
with his own convictions. If he did not find four such men in
the summer of 1953, he found at least one in the new chairman, Admiral Arthur W. Radford, dynamic and able Commander in Chief of the Pacific Fleet.

Whether Mr. Eisenhower expected from the beginning to
work primarily with Admiral Radford or not, this quickly
became the pattern. Radford recalls that at the beginning of
his term "the President told me never to hesitate to speak up,
even though I was not a member [of the National Security
Council], at any time in the course of the meeting on any
subject that I thought was of importance. I did that. In other
words, that was an independent action that I could take,
without necessarily warning the Secretary of Defense in advance." [60] The Chairman of the Joint Chiefs of Staff became
over the period of the next four years the source of a single
authoritative military judgment, not because of the statutory
powers of the chairman, which were designed to preclude
this, and not because of the support of the Secretary of
Defense (which was altogether beside the point), but because
he conducted himself almost without exception in harmony
with the convictions of the Commander in Chief. This is not
a case of sycophancy, but a rare case of mutuality for which
there is little in the way of Congressional remedies. The Joint
Chiefs of Staff during the Radford term have been assailed
(as an institution) with such vehemence and from such

quarters as to be a matter of some interest. Mr. Eisenhower is first among the critics. Apparently expecting them to "make budget decisions," he complains that these decisions devolved upon civilians because internal differences in the JCS "tended to neutralize the advisory influence they should have enjoyed as a body." [61] The Rockefeller Panel Report in 1958 referred to them as "a committee of partisan adversaries." [62] Professor Hammond has been particularly harsh: they are "essentially spokesmen of the interests and perspectives of their services," who leave premises unexplored, oversimplify nonmilitary factors, maintain a barrier against everyone and anyone and, worst of all, do "not want outsiders to know too much about their work." [63] Mr. Eisenhower and Mr. Rockefeller had a number of specific remedies in mind to overcome the malaise which they incorporated in the 1958 Reorganization Act proposals.

Neil H. McElroy

The four and one-half years of "Engine Charlie" Wilson at the Pentagon were an eventful prelude for the climactic two years that followed. Neil Hosler McElroy, President of Procter and Gamble, arrived at the Pentagon with Sputnik and, according to anonymous sources at the time, remained in orbit thereafter. The plight of McElroy is worth pondering. There is absolutely no evidence that he either sought or wanted the post of Secretary of Defense. Rather the evidence is that he did not want it and accepted the post only to accommodate a man he greatly admired. There was, reportedly, an agreement that McElroy would serve for two years only. This was later complicated by the fact that the President became seriously committed to McElroy's finishing out the term of the administration. McElroy did not have the background of a major defense industry to prepare him for his strange role; his whole career had been one of the promotion and sales of soap. Consequently, he entered not only into a situation of major strategic decisions with which he was unfamiliar but into wholly new administrative processes. When he returned to Cincinnati late in 1959, after the two years he had reluctantly promised the President, the experience, if it had not unnerved McElroy (and there is no evidence for that), had shaken as hardened an observer of the Pentagon scene as *Fortune's* Charles J. V. Murphy: "It is no secret," wrote Murphy, "that the circumstances of McElroy's going home vexed and embarrassed the President . . . It is also no secret that McElroy's second year in the Pentagon failed to match the superb promise of the first . . . His recent performance has confirmed the conclusion that the defense job is far too important in itself, far too deeply enmeshed in the other processes of government and national policy, ever again to be given to a man who has not already served an apprenticeship under pressure in Washington and preferably in the field of defense and strategy."[64] While these words will be noted for their overall lack of prophetic value, they did, of course, describe Thomas Sovereign Gates, Jr., McElroy's immediate successor.

In October 1957 the budget cycle for fiscal year 1959 was underway, and McElroy was able to take to Congress early in 1958 increased requests which reflected not so much the thinking of the new secretary as the temperature level of the Congress,which was still very much in the throes of Sputnik fever. The Preparedness Subcommittee of the Senate Armed Services Committee, under Lyndon B. Johnson, was well into a major investigation of U.S. missile capability. From this point on, McElroy was caught up in a maelstrom of strategy and weapons that was barely comprehensible to him. The Russian space effort and the approaching presidential election provided the outer environment for a new wrangle on missiles, bombers, submarines, limited war, general war, and so on. The pleasant, mild-mannered man from Cincinnati found the language of the Congress "spooky,"[65] although in some measure it was his own language which got the missile-gap controversy rather badly out of perspective. McElroy's presentations to Congress by way of what the Soviets "could" do in missile production aroused a host of adversaries, among them an old antagonist of Secretaries of Defense, Senator Stuart Symington of Missouri. It was not difficult to arouse the senator; as one observer put it, "all Symington ever really wanted was more of everything."

However, the Eisenhower administration was well informed throughout the 1958-1960 period about Soviet capabilities in the intercontinental- and intermediate-range missile fields—better informed than it was prepared to relate to Congress in order to protect increasingly effective means of intelligence access. The Soviets were preoccupied with an intermediate-range ballistic missile (IRBM) capability aimed at Western Europe and had not embarked on either a long-range bomber or a long-range missile deployment. Mr. Eisenhower refused to launch a crash program of missile production, reiterating the validity of two points: proceeding cautiously in a highly volatile and new technological realm, and the necessity for maintaining a "mix" of strategic delivery systems. Both the President and the Pentagon were aware of the magnitude of the investment in Strategic Air Command bombers and emphasized that the B-52 would be the mainstay of strategic nuclear war well into the 1960s. Plans were underway to phase out medium-range B-47 bombers and to withdraw from forward bases overseas. At the same time, the United States was already committed to a versatile, if cautious, missile program. ATLAS and TITAN systems had been under a presidential priority since 1955 and were scheduled for operational deployment by 1960. Second-generation, solid-fuel systems (MINUTEMAN and PO-LARIS) were under development with the Navy's marriage of the nuclear-powered submarine and the nuclear-tipped, solid-fuel missle, the outstanding achievement of the century in weapons technology. This situation which presumably could have been turned to good use by one who had been deeply involved in it throughout the 1950s was outside the ken of Mr. McElroy. [66]

President Eisenhower transmitted to Congress on April 3, 1958, his most far-reaching proposals for the reorganization of the Department of Defense.[67] The proposals embodied the essentials of the Eisenhower-Rockefeller concept of the role of the Secretary of Defense. Secretary of Defense McElroy, called upon to lay the proposals before Congress, was little more than a bystander in their development and in the ensuing controversy between the armed services committees and the President. Eisenhower proceeded from the premise that "separate ground, air, and sea warfare is gone forever." This dictated first that the planning and execution of strategy and operations be vested in "the mechanism of the Secretary of Defense and the Joint Chiefs of Staff." Avoiding language of a single service or, for that matter, of a single chief of staff, the President proposed the establishment of Unified Commands reporting directly to the Secretary of Defense, thereby removing "operations" from the three services and their civilian secretaries. This move would require that the Secretary of Defense have greatly enhanced financial and budgetary "flexibility." The President's letter of transmittal suggested to the Congress that he was calling for a single-sum appropriation for the Secretary of Defense, to be allocated by him in turn on a functional rather than service basis. Mr. Eisenhower was quite clear in his request for authority for the Secretary of Defense to "transfer, reassign, abolish or consolidate" service functions. Yet in a press conference on April 9, 1958, the President hastened to correct any "misinterpretations" that he was calling for a "lump-sum" appropriation, insisting only on "financial flexibility" for the secretary.[68]

The dean of Congressional overseers of defense, Representative Carl Vinson, Chairman of the House Armed Services Committee, was persuaded that the President was undertaking what had been specifically prohibited since 1947—the merger of the armed forces, if not directly, then indirectly through the device of extraordinary powers for the Secretary of Defense. This was precisely the development James Forrestal had feared would ensue. There was also the consideration, of equal concern to Vinson, that the President was assaulting fundamental prerogatives of the Congress to "control the purse and the sword." The Georgia "Swamp Fox" struck out at both aspects of the proposal: "Concentration of military control, subject to the mental and physical capabilities of one individual secretary . . . is an open invitation to the concept of the man on horseback . . . [Moreover], the President has asked Congress to surrender to one man in the Pentagon its constitutional responsibility to prescribe the basic roles and missions for the armed services . . . he has directed the Department of Defense to prepare its budget in such a way as to reduce the Congress' control over appropriations of funds for defense purposes."[69] The "man on horseback" that both Forrestal and Vinson feared most was a civilian, not a soldier. The Reorganization Act of 1958, which passed the Senate only some three months after its introduction, permitted the Secretary of Defense to *transfer functions,* but not to abolish any of the services. Full details of such transfers would have to be reported to the two armed services committees thirty days in advance. Ries sees the Congress having kept open alternatives in maintaining the separate services: "If Congress had permitted the elimination of the separate service departments . . . by allowing the Secretary to destroy them by transferring or consolidating their functions, Congress would lose its only meaningful tool of control, alternatives. Three separate departments with overlapping functions would generate alternatives."[70] But if the administration had been handed a defeat on this issue, it was only a partial defeat.

James Forrestal had concluded that the "general" authority of the Secretary of Defense needed to be clarified in such a way as to give him undisputed "control" of the Department of Defense. In this sense, both Lovett and Gates approved of a strengthening of the position of the secretary.

None of the three, however, sought to concentrate in the office of the Secretary of Defense the operational functions of the military establishment. "Control," not "operations," was the meaning of the authority sought by them. Testifying in support of the Eisenhower-Rockefeller proposals, Secretary McElroy declared that the provisions of the National Security Act, which allowed for the separate administration of the services, did not permit the Secretary of Defense complete "operating" authority. McElroy was proposing that the authority of the Secretary of Defense be defined in such a way that through the assistant secretaries he could control functional areas which heretofore had been service responsibilities. This indeed had already been accomplished in budgeting. The burden of the Eisenhower-Rockefeller thesis being argued by McElroy was that the overall management and operation of the defense apparatus should lie in the office of the Secretary of Defense; otherwise the secretary's authority would constantly be in question.[71] Ries comments that "Secretary McElroy saw the authority of the Assistant Secretaries as intimately involved in his own authority. If his authority was to be effective, he must be able to delegate it to his Assistant Secretaries . . . The Assistant Secretaries were extensions of the personality of the Secretary of Defense. When they acted, they acted in his name. When they spoke, they spoke with his voice. When they exercised authority, they exercised his authority."[72]

The secretary addressed himself specifically to the question of weapons research and development already under the jurisdiction of an Assistant Secretary of Defense. But the difficulty was that the authority of the Secretary of Defense in this area was not clear. He told the Senate Committee on Armed Services that the present assistant secretary could not "give orders." McElroy proposed a civilian Director of Defense Research and Engineering who would be responsible for all scientific and technical matters pertaining to weapons development for all the services. The director would have authority to supervise *and direct* all research and engineering activities. Thereby this functional area would become part of the central management of the Department of Defense. There was also the unavoidable implication that civilian management at the level of the office of the Secretary of Defense could better make weapons decisions for the three services than their own civilian and professional military leaders could make. Insofar as there is a concept of delegation and sharing present in these proposals, it is one of sharing among alter egos within the office of the Secretary of Defense. It is the antithesis of the concept of delegation down into the services of Forrestal-Lovett-Gates. "Functionalism" emerges as the antithesis of the "generalist" concept. Congress approved the position of Director Defense Research and Engineering and struck out the language of "separately administered" services, trusting that "separately organized" military departments would preserve for it the necessary alternatives. Ries, however, concludes at this point that for Congress the battle had been lost: "the National Security Act of 1958 made possible for the Department of Defense the indirect accomplishment of what it had been specifically denied since 1948 . . . the Secretary could consolidate and assign to an organization entity he deemed appropriate all service and support activities common to more than one service." [73]

Sweeping though it may have been, the 1958 reorganization did not, to use Secretary McElroy's phrase, remove all "the sand in the gearbox." The Eisenhower-Rockefeller concept of the role of the Secretary of Defense was far from being fully contained in the latest National Security Act or, it may be said, in the person of Mr. McElroy. Governor Rockefeller spelled out to the Jackson Subcommittee on National Policy Machinery in 1960 what remained to be done: "further reorganization of the Defense Department to achieve unified doctrine, planning, and command" was required, a recommendation that clearly put him at odds with Secretary Gates. Rockefeller continued:

More specifically this means the following: (a) The Chairman of the Joint Chiefs of Staff should be designated principal military advisor to the Secretary of Defense and the President, and be responsible for the development of overall strategic doctrine. (b) The Staff of the Joint Chiefs should be organized on a unified basis under the direct authority of the Chairman. (c) All officers above the rank of brigadier general or the equivalent should be designed officers of the Armed Forces of the United States—not [of] the individual service of their earlier careers—and their promotion should be placed in the control of the Department of Defense. (d) Full authority should be given to the Secretary of Defense over all military research, development, and procurement, so that he may assure the most productive utilization of research and development funds. (e) The budget process of the Department of Defense should be revised so that the Congress appropriates all funds to the Secretary, thereby fixing in him a focus of fiscal responsibility similar to that held by other departments.[74]

As if by design, Rockefeller was resurrecting every "sore-point" left over from fifteen years of controversy. The proposal to put the defense budget "in the name of the Secretary of Defense," so that he could personally allocate funds on a functional basis, had been emphatically rejected only two years before. While it had not been brought up in 1958, Rockefeller also emphasized the principle of "a single chief of staff." He would first of all separate the Chiefs from their services, so that they would not have to get "approval of every move" from their services, and produce one strategic doctrine rather than four. However, the Chiefs would merely be "advisory"; the chairman would be the principal assistant to the President and the secretary with full responsibility for strategic plans and operations.[75] In this position he was supported by General Maxwell Taylor, Army Chief of Staff from 1955 to 1959, who was now busily writing from the vantage point of retirement.[76]

The most likely model of "a single chief," Admiral Arthur W. Radford, was more reserved on the question. Ultimately, the Chiefs may have to be separated from the services, he thought, although the present system seemed to be working well now (that is, under Secretary Gates). Radford was not prepared, however, to support the principle of one man having full strategic and operational responsibility. Moreover, he was emphatically opposed to Rockefeller's suggestions about the Joint Staff and promotions.[77] Rockefeller wanted the "allegiance and responsibility" of the top-ranking officers to be to the executive agent, the central authority, namely, the Department of Defense, and not to the individual services. The latter were "divisive factors," and steps needed to be taken to overcome the "natural and very logical" tendencies of officers toward their services.[78] On the fusionist theme of joint State-Defense staffs, Rockefeller could not muster any support from such members of the Eisenhower administration as Secretary of State Christian A. Herter, General Cutler, Secretary Gates, or Admiral Radford. Invariably the men who had spent years in the national security apparatus rejected the suggestion as unrealistic.

Two Role Concepts

The first seven Secretaries of Defense served just over thirteen years in office. In directing attention to five of them, we have found that in order to adequately encompass their various understandings of the role of the Secretary of Defense two formulations are necessary. Our purpose has been to establish the intellectual bank derived from the experience of previous secretaries which was available to Mr. McNamara in 1961. We can conclude this undertaking by making as full an explication of the two role concepts as possible.

The result of the conclusions of James V. Forrestal, Robert A. Lovett, and Thomas S. Gates is a *generalist* role for the Secretary of Defense. The viewpoint of this role concept may be described as objectivist-realist. That is to say, it arises inductively from experience for the most part; it is notably bare of preconceptions and illusion. It is reserved and taciturn about men and human judgment; at the same time it provides a certain witness to the variety of human accomplishment. The objective factors which impinge most sharply on this conceptualization of the secretary's role are policy, professionalism, and responsibility. The foremost reality in the generalist role concept is the primacy of policy. Policy is the heart of the political function of national leadership. The Secretary of Defense must participate in and be concerned with the establishment of effective policy processes. Not only must policy rest on an objective assessment of the present-day world, it must also be made operative through processes which have proved practicable in the experience of men who have been associated with and responsible for policy. It is a question not of the need for clarity in the directives by which the military establishment will be guided but of the achievement of clarity and understanding through the effective participation of civilians and military in the policy process.

The preoccupation of the Secretary of Defense in the generalist formulation is with policy. This leads to the second factor—his recognition of the integrity of professionalism. In defining "objective civilian control," Huntington suggests that the essence of it is the recognition of autonomous military professionalism. He argues that "the most subtle and persuasive form which liberal anti-militarism could assume" would be to enjoin the Joint Chiefs of Staff to "fuse" ideological, scientific, political, and military thinking in their determinations.[79] There is, of course, a pluralism of professions in the national security policy process, with the professionalism of the military the most basic—after that of the national political leadership. Scientific, technological, economic, medical-psychological, and many other professional competences are brought to bear in this realm. The generalist secretary will not portray or represent any one of these, but will take account of and rely on all, recognizing again the unique province of the military. Judgments must be rendered at the levels of policy, strategy, resource allocation, and military operations. The secretary is responsible for the coordination and integration of judgments at each level. The responsibility of the Secretary of Defense is the final consideration in the generalist role concept. The position of the secretary will be defined by his responsibilities, not by his functions, by his overall control of the system, not by the degree of his direct involvement. Such a role requires ample authority, but adequate authority is not equated in this view with functional consolidation in the secretary.

A *functionalist* role for the Secretary of Defense represents the conclusions of President Eisenhower and Mr. Rockefeller, as well as the practice of Mr. Wilson and Mr. McElroy. The functionalist role concept of the Secretary of Defense has been imposed on the national military establishment from the outside. It derives, by and large, from three external sources: from a "former military person" and President with explicit views about command and staff arrangements and a popular ideological view of civil-military relations; from a "reform-minded" scion of industrial wealth of the classic Tory-Liberal mold; and from American corporate industry with its strong flavor of functional management. Inasmuch as the functionalist viewpoint is a product of environmental factors and has been brought to the national military establishment, and inasmuch as it represents a distillation of the American liberal ethos on questions of foreign policy, civil-military relations, reform administration, and private enterprise, it may be characterized "subjectivist" or "ideological."

The Secretary of Defense, in keeping with the structure and tenets of American industry, will have management as his primary concern. American corporations not known for their decentralization provide one overriding principle: the consolidation of management authority in a single executive. Through the agency of efficient management, effective national security measures will be produced. All participants must join in the commitment to efficient implementation of policy, which has been set outside the management apparatus but which will be carried forward according to management tenets. Inasmuch as decisions and direction are vested in the secretary, the functions of the Department of Defense are to be vested in him as well. The elaboration of the authority of the secretary is equated with the clustering of functions in the office of the secretary and his direct participation in them. Under the rubric of management, he becomes *primus inter pares* in each functional-professional group which subjects its judgments to his own as a prior step to coordination and integration. The ultimate responsibility of coordination and integration of judgments becomes a process for the secretary of coordinating his own various judgments as major participant in each functional role. The broader policy determinants are the prerogative of the President, who will be advised by whomsoever he may call upon.

The assumption, again, is that "it is the men," not organizational blueprints or prescriptions, who are crucial in tracing the evolution of the role of the Secretary of Defense. At bottom, an attitude, an inner conviction about men, distinguishes those who would adhere to the generalist role, just as an equally distinct outlook marks those who would reject it for the participant role of the functionalist. The attitude of the latter is aggressive, not reserved, confident, not restrained; it is given to producing friction and tension, not to seeking accomodation and balance. It is brash and brilliant, not wise or judicious. The two role concepts with two basic dispositions underlying them are inherently divergent. Mr. McNamara would not specifically employ either; rather he would undertake to meld them.

2
The New Management

 President-elect John F. Kennedy's Committee on the Defense Establishment reported one month after his election with recommendations for further reorganization of the Department of Defense.[1] In view of the vigorous role played in defense matters for more than a decade by the committee chairman, Senator Stuart Symington, the recommendations were not surprising. Symington and the committee asked for a single chief of staff supported by a military advisory council, for additional "functional" commands, and for the abolition of the service secretaries with their functions to accrue to the Secretary of of Defense. If the President-elect was ever disposed toward the Symington Committee recommendations, it was before he met Robert Strange McNamara.

Robert S. McNamara was elected President of the Ford Motor Company on November 9, 1960, at the age of forty-four after some fourteen years in Ford management. (It is probably not useful to push any parallels with John F. Kennedy beyond this point.) McNamara came to Washington relatively unknown but with strong convictions about "techniques of administration" and their applicability to the Department of Defense. Immediately recognized as persuasive and forceful, he succeeded in tabling the Symington Committee Report. McNamara argued that the introduction of a new mode of management would more effectively achieve full "direction, authority and control" in the Secretary of Defense than would further reorganization of the department. Charles J. Hitch has indicated something of what the the new secretary had in mind: "Robert S. McNamara made it clear from the beginning that he intended to be the kind of Secretary that President Eisenhower had in mind in 1958." That is to say, McNamara intended to exert the kind of "initiative" Eisenhower desired in the Secretary of Defense. The "reforms" McNamara had in mind, however, were of a different order than those contained in the Eisenhower-Rockefeller schema. H. Struve Hensel's contention in 1954 that "the trend away from centralization is both clear and irresistable" would not stand as an example of prophecy.[2] Mr. Kennedy was wholly prepared at the outset of his administration to avoid a round of reorganization hearings. Robert S. McNamara became the eighth Secretary of Defense in January 1961.

The new management mode consisted (1) of a set of basic premises which set the intellectual stance of the McNamara group and (2) of management tools which established the working methodology. The premises would be more significant than the tools. Mr. McNamara was aware that "control over the premises of decision" and an insistence upon "rationality" would do more to insure "correct" decisions than would any adjustments in the structure of organization.[3] He chose to exert his greatest influence on the decision-making process in the Department of Defense in this manner. The introduction of new management techniques had the singular purpose of facilitating decisions and guaranteeing rational processes. Given the premises, there would be "an inexorable logic" to the decision-making process so long as the secretary maintained firm control over both premises and tools. In this chapter our purpose is to examine some of the most important of these and point up their impact. We will find that they are not entirely the product of Mr. McNamara's active mind; an extraordinary group of like-minded associates played an important role as well.

Active Management

"President Kennedy's charge to me was a dual one," Mr. McNamara has written, "to determine what forces were required and to procure and support them as economically as possible."[4] The charge was accepted with relish; it provided a supreme opportunity (he had been President of Ford only forty-two days) to execute a concept of management which he was convinced the Department of Defense required. Mr. McNamara reached the conclusion early that the "mechanism of decision-making [in the Department of Defense] left something to be desired . . . We had to begin with a thorough re-examination and analysis of the contingencies we might face around the world. I considered that we were *too slow* to develop the alternatives and the decisions as to the numbers and types of forces we *really needed* . . . To be really meaningful the defense program must be looked at in its entirety, with each of its elements considered in light of the total program. This can be done only at the Department of Defense level."[5] Among the new civilian heads of the Department of Defense there was the conviction that "active management at the top" could achieve the desired goals of speeding up the decision-making process and determining the real military requirements of the nation. The McNamara "philosophy of management" was designed for the occasion. In language that recalls the terminology of the 1953 Rockefeller Committee Report, Secretary McNamara relates that

When I became Secretary of Defense in 1961, I felt that either of two broad philosophies of management could be followed by the man at the head of this great establishment. He could play an essentially passive role—a judicial role. In this role the Secretary would make the decisions required of him by law by approving recommendations made to him. On the other hand, the Secretary of Defense could play an active role providing aggressive leadership—questioning, suggesting alternatives, proposing objectives and stimulating progress. This active role represents my own philosophy of management. I became convinced that there was room for and need of this kind of management philosophy in the Department of Defense.[6]

Active management at the top has suggested to many, including Mr. McNamara's first comptroller, that there is "an inevitable tendency in bureaucracies for decisions to be made at higher and higher levels."[7] In responding to this theme, the secretary engages in an interesting transition of thought: "I strongly believe in the pyramid nature of decision-making and that within that frame, decision-making should be pushed to the lowest level in the organization *that has the ability and information available to apply approved policy . . . Our effort has been to create a framework of policy within which meaningful decentralization of operations can be accomplished.*"[8] There are, first of all, reservations about decentralization of decision-making; thereafter, it is not clear whether the secretary is speaking of the decentralization of policy decisions or the decentralization of "execution" (operations). Perhaps there is some clarification of his thought when he states at another point that "my effort has been to provide our military leaders and my civilian associates . . . the best factual basis for judgment which can be produced."[9] Decisions are taken on the basis of information available, but they are, in the final analysis, the result of "judgments." Mr. McNamara's philosophy of active management addresses itself cautiously to the judgmental element of decision-making, as we shall see.

In the endeavor to put the decision-making process on a "rational foundation," Mr. McNamara has argued that "judgments" can no longer be "intuitive," nor can they be based on past "experience" alone. McNamara is somewhat paradoxical on the issue. He insists on the one hand that judgment can only facilitate decision "if the philosophy of active management is to be followed," and on the other hand that he would not, if he could, substitute "analytical techniques for judgment based on experience." At the same time he stresses that the requirement for a broader factual basis for judgment necessitates the introduction of "the analytical technique" and increasing reliance on "sophisticated analyses." [10] Mr. Alain G. Enthoven, initially Deputy Assistant Secretary (Systems Analysis) and later assistant secretary, confirms, that the entire office of the Secretary of Defense was undertaking the development of a "new analytical approach" for synthesizing the elements of defense planning. Enthoven stressed that "it is appropriate that the broader application of the analytical approach be led by the Secretary of Defense because an important part of his job is to stimulate innovation and reform." [11] So-called "direct experience" and "reading history books" might have been sufficient for the military planner at one time, but today, according to Mr. Enthoven, in order to assess the relevancy of accumulated experience, it is necessary to apply "the careful rules of scientific method." [12] Testifying before the Defense Subcommittee of the House Appropriations Committee, McNamara stated that "the basic objective of the management system we are introducing and trying to operate, is to establish a *rational foundation* as opposed to an *emotional foundation* for the decisons as to what size force and what type of force this country will maintain. This rational structure, this intellectual foundation . . . is something that is laid out on paper." [13]

The Deputy Assistant Secretary for Systems Analysis could not fail to take note of the fact that the effort to establish a "rational" foundation had, itself, become an "emotional" matter. He observed in an address to the Naval War College in June 1963 that "Sometimes Defense gets to be a pretty emotional business. Many people involved have strong feelings about it, and that is not at all surprising . . . Although inevitably some people will resent the application of dispassionate, cold analysis to something as rich in meaning and tradition as warfare and strategy, there is no sensible alternative in the nuclear age . . . We must make defense planning and the selection of weapon systems an intellectual rather than an emotional process."[14] The strains within the Defense Department in mid-1963 were showing through in Enthoven's remarks (the McClellan Hearings on the TFX contract were reaching a peak). Before a well-chosen audience, he abjured those "proponents of some programs indulging whatever prejudices they have" who would "fight for their favorite weapon system because it symbolizes a way of life." Warming to his subject, Enthoven saw himself and his associates confronted by a host of unscientific adversaries who were endangering "the effective pursuit of our national security objectivies." But the way out was clear. "The question is whether . . . judgments have to be made in the fog of inadequate and inaccurate data, unclear and undefined issues, and a welter of conflicting personal opinions, or whether they can be made on the basis of adequate, reliable information, relevant experience, and clearly drawn issues . . . In the balance between reliance on authority and experience, the tug of vested interests, and the scientific method, I believe we need more scientific method."[15] A year later Mr. Enthoven was not completely calm. He told the aviation and space writers that he wished differences in the Department of Defense would not be described so frequently as resulting from "emotion, partisan politics, parochialism, narrowness, arrogance, downgrading somebody or what have you!"[16] The Secretary of Defense was surprised to find how sensitive the methodology issue was, but he remained adamant about the application of what he called "quantitative common sense."

The premise of active management at the top is more sweeping than it might appear. It puts the Secretary of Defense firmly in control of the overall process of decision-making which can be summarized as follows: *a policy framework is set by the secretary; much of the data base is provided by the secretary; judgments are invited by the secretary; decisions are made by the secretary.* In a word, power is concentrated in the Secretary of Defense under a philosophy of active management.[17] The workings of this decision-making process will be illustrated in two subsequent chapters; at this point it is necessary to look at the second major premise of the McNamara group.

The Economic Criterion

The terms and categories of economic analysis provided the model of rational decision-making for Mr. McNamara. Economics is concerned with the allocation of resources ("choosing doctrines and techniques") and the most efficient use of resources. Efficiency, in turn, is a common denominator that cuts across strategy, technology, and economy. Strategy, technology, and economy are not three independent "considerations"; they are interdependent elements of the single problem of efficient use of resources. Under the rubric of "efficiency," military decisions can be understood as economic decisions. Two factors, which impinge on the defense problem as never before, make this way of looking at military decision-making critical. They are "scarcity of resources" and "technological proliferation." The revolution in military technology has so increased the range of choice and the number of alternatives that "a pre-World War II decision-making mechanism" is no longer adequate. "Our problems of choice among alternatives in strategy and in weapon systems have been complicated enormously by the bewildering array of entirely workable alternative courses which our technology can support," contends Mr. McNamara.[18] The phenomenon of technological acceleration on an unprecedented scale might strike some as belying scarcity of resources. Quite the contrary, the world of the decision-maker is "a world in which resources are limited." The fact of a luxury of choice counterposed against a dearth of resources demands that choices be made under the constraint of economy. It is emphasized that "In the face of the expanding number of systems that we could buy, we have not escaped the ancient necessity of choice, arising out of the scarcity of available resources. Whether we like it or not, in the United States today, we have only a limited amount of goods and services available at any one time . . . therefore, we have to choose." Enthoven adds, "Choosing strategies and weapon systems is fundamentally an economic problem, using the term in its precise sense. That is, it is a problem in choosing how best to use our limited dollars and limited resources . . . To do this properly, one must think through the purposes of the weapon system, formulate good criteria of effectiveness, and then consider alternative systems or mixes of systems in terms of their effectiveness or cost." It must be noted that while "scarcity of resources" is stipulated as a major justification for the new management by Mr. McNamara, he has repeatedly emphasized that there is "no limit" upon the amount that might be spent on national security. [19]

Economic analysis or economic choice is anything but esoteric. What is important is the comparison of all relevant alternatives, in terms of the objectives that each can accomplish and in terms of the costs of each. The selection of the best alternative—it may be only a "good" alternative—is done on the basis of an *economic criterion*. Strategies are merely ways of using resources; technology tells us, in turn, what strategies are possible. But economy does not turn out to be simply a third element in a problem that will be subjected to a higher test. Economy is the test; economy decides. Hitch explains as follows:

By "criterion" we mean *the test* by which we choose one alternative or system rather than another. The choice of an appropriate economic criterion is frequently the central problem in designing a systems analysis. In principle, the criterion we want is clear enough: the optimal system is the one which yields the greatest excess of positive values (objectives) over negative values (resources used up, or costs) . . . Military decisions, whether they specifically involve budgetary allocations or not, are in *one of their important aspects economic decisions;* and . . . unless the right questions are asked, the appropriate alternatives selected for comparison, and an *economic criterion* used for choosing, the most efficient military power and national security will suffer.[20]

Consequently, before an alternative weapon system or objective is chosen, the criterion of choice must be chosen. While Hitch has insisted that "judgment is always of critical importance in designing the analysis, choosing the alternatives to be compared, and *selecting the criterion,*" it is invariably a matter of choosing *the most appropriate economic criterion.* [21]

Charles J. Hitch, who had been a RAND Corporation economist before serving some four and one-half years as comptroller under Mr. McNamara, has been a major theorist of the new management. He has supplied many of the basic axioms which tend to strike one as at once unassailable and doubtful. Maxims such as "the choice of a particular strategy or military objective cannot be divorced from the cost of achieving it," or "the military worth of a weapon system cannot be considered in isolation, it must be considered in relation to its cost," are innocuous enough if one can cost out a weapon system, not to mention a strategy. However, the following are of a somewhat different order: private consumer choices and weapons procurement rest on "exactly the same principle," and military requirements are meaningful "only in terms of benefits to be gained in relation to costs." [22] The difficulty with these propositions is that Hitch can be quoted against himself by them without the end result of any significant reconciliation. Before coming to the Pentagon, he was particularly acute on the interrelationship of technology and economy. "In economics we distinguish between the problem of allocating resources efficiently within a given technology and the problem of advancing technology . . . Economic theory has a great deal more to say about the static allocation problem than about the promotion of technological progress which is . . . less tractable to analysis."[23] Nonetheless, the appropriate function of research and development planning, says Hitch, is to "develop a strategy for broadly advancing the state of the technological art in areas of relevance to national security." But, again, strategies may be thought of simply as ways to use resources, to exploit the existing technology. Here Mr. McNamara's convictions are critical, for it is he who controls the premises, not the comptroller. It is fundamental to the new management that the issues be posed in such a way as to be tractable to analysis. A "measured and orderly" approach is essential to a "rational" system. Stability is enhanced by confining choices within an already prolific technology. Moreover, the scarcity of resources impinges on any decision. Hitch conceded recently that Mr. McNamara did not approach the defense problem only in terms of "getting the most defense from a given level of resources"; the amount of resources allocated to defense is itself an issue with the secretary as well.[24] There is some paradox in the fact that Hitch established a financial management system oriented to "outputs," while Mr. McNamara's orientation was to "inputs" or "resources consumed."

The Programming Function

Two analytical tools, or management techniques, have been most characteristic of the new management mode and have gone farthest to implement Mr. McNamara's premises: these are "programming" within the broader schema of planning-programming-budgeting and "cost-effectiveness analyses." To understand the McNamara role concept it is necessary to understand his employment of these particular techniques. In our treatment of them we will follow most closely the accounts of Mr. Hitch and Mr. Enthoven as well as that of the Secretary of Defense. Because the tools of the new management are so central to the theoretical and practical mode of the McNamara group, there is a marked sensitivity to criticism of them. In his "epilogue," Mr. Hitch, for example, is willing to note that not all objectives had been reached and that in certain instances he now sees the wisdom of some of the old ways; but he stoutly hurls back all assaults on programming and cost-effectiveness analyses. This contrasts with a more reserved treatment of such tools in the "prologue." Substantial critics have raised serious questions about their validity, nonetheless, and attention will be directed to this criticism. [25]

The programming function is at the heart of the financial management system installed in the Department of Defense by Comptroller Hitch at the direction of Secretary McNamara. Its advent is explained in part by the McNamara group's perception of the procedures of its predecessors. The group noted that after the tenure of Secretary Lovett a dichotomy between planning and budgeting had developed in the department. Planning was "militarized" and budgeting was "civilianized." What was not perceptible was any "bridge" between the two functions. Directing himself to the budgeting function, Mr. Hitch has suggested that the primary method used by civilians, prior to 1961, to bring the budget into line with administration fiscal policies "was to divide a total defense budget ceiling among the three military departments, leaving to each department, by and large, the allocation of its ceiling among its own functions, units, and activities." This might suggest that budgeting was not entirely "civilianized," but Hitch's point (not without its patronizing overtones) is that "the Defense Secretaries used this method because they lacked the management techniques needed to do it any other way." [26] To point up the "greatest weakness" in this approach to budgeting, Hitch returns to the theme of the revolution in military technology. "The great technical complexity of modern-day weapons, their lengthy period of development, their tremendous combat power, and their

enormous cost have placed an extraordinary premium on the
sound choice of major weapon systems in relation to tasks
and missions and our national security objectives. These
choices have become, for the top management of the Defense
Department, the key decisions around which much of the
Defense program revolves."[27] What a modern financial management system must do above all else, then, is "relate"
weapons systems, tasks, and objectives to costs. It must
"bridge" the planning and budgeting functions. This, Hitch
contends, was not done prior to 1961. More importantly,
because of the lack of a comprehensive financial system in
the past, the Secretary of Defense and the "top management" had not been making the critical decisions. The introduction of the programming function into the financial management system would be the means for putting the
"initiative" and the decisions in the hands of the Secretary of
Defense. Although this was done, it should be pointed out
that during the McNamara years the defense budget was
divided between the three services in the same percentage
terms as before (the Vietnam buildup in 1965 excluded).

The financial management system (FMS) of the Department of Defense must succeed in achieving five goals, according to the comptroller. It is precisely these goals that dictate
the structure of the system. The FMS must produce a budget
in a form acceptable to Congress, account for funds in the
same manner in which they are appropriated, provide managers at all levels of the department with necessary information, and produce financial information required by other
governmental agencies. But the overriding objective is to produce data needed by top defense management for decision-
making on force levels, weapons, and so on, "in the form
desired." The last objective is a new objective and requires
the new function of programming in what will now be a
three-phased system.

Wilfred J. McNeil, architect of the pre-1961 financial
management system, voiced strong objections to Hitch's

proposals from the outset and suggested that they were more substantial than concerns with "accounting difficulties." McNeil told the Jackson Subcommittee in 1961:

> The principle of making appropriations for the Department of Defense based on full funding of either complete programs or usable increments of a program is sound and should be continued. Only in this way will there be either within the Department or in the Congress an opportunity to grasp and understand the magnitude of the programs under consideration. Congressional and departmental control can only be exercised in advance of undertaking the program and not later at the time the liability is to be liquidated and a check to be written. I am emphasizing this point because in the past it has been proposed and in the future Congress may again be urged to make appropriations on the so-called expenditure basis. Certainly the rate of expenditure is a vital consideration, but real control must be exercised before a project is undertaken or the obligation is created and not afterward. I would urge that the Congress be wary of proposals for any change in this basic principle of making appropriations and I believe the experience of the Appropriations Committee will support this observation. At this point I might add that the so-called package plan does not provide a suitable basis for an appropriation structure. I will repeat, it is one method of evaluating major weapons systems.[28]

Hitch admits to changing his mind on another aspect of the McNeil system after some experience with it, that is, on the categories stipulated for the defense budget and for the appropriations accounts. The budget is set by statute in terms of "input" or "resource" categories, not in terms of "output" or "mission" categories—thus: (1) Military Personnel, (2) Operation and Maintenance, (3) Procurement, (4) Research and Development, and (5) Military Construction. Hitch at first wished to bring the budget into line with the categories of his FMS which were "output" categories. He now recognizes certain advantages of the present budget structure, not the least of which is that Congress wants it that way. In any case, the problem of "converting" input and output data to statutory categories is within the capability of the FMS. Finally, on the matter of supplying information to other government agencies, the picture is not entirely clear. Secretary McNamara emphasized in 1961 that he was working closely with the Bureau of the Budget but emphasized with perhaps more vigor in 1965 that the Bureau of the Budget was not making any decisions that had anything to do with the Department of Defense. It was clear, at any rate, that the bureau did not have the hold on the McNamara Pentagon that it had on other agencies.

Hitch had projected eighteen months as the time required to put a new financial management system into operation. Mr. McNamara reduced this to six months so that his first budget (fiscal year 1963) could be based on it. What cannot be emphasized too much is the extent and impact of the comptroller's role at this juncture. He is not instituting a new budget, but rather a comprehensive planning-programming-budgeting system. Throughout 1961 Hitch established entirely new terms of discourse in planning and in budgeting, but more significantly he introduced the programming function as the conversion element connecting the two. In order to provide "top management" with the data they desire, *in the form desired,* new terms of reference are imposed. It would be the responsibility of the comptroller to stand guard over the defense discourse. There is merely an aspect of the comptroller's role in an official description that states he will develop "measures of resource utilizations and methods of characterizing resource limitations and availabilities."[29] We shall return to this point after outlining "Mr. Hitch's marvelous budget-making machine."[30]

"Planning" is the first phase of the three-phased McNamara-Hitch financial management system. The traditional military planning function and determination of requirements are by no means the definition of this phase. From the standpoint of the FMS, the emphasis in this phase is on the review of requirements by top management. Since the preparation of the fiscal year 1957 budget (1955-56), planning had centered on the preparation of the Joint Strategic Objectives Plan (JSOP) in the Joint Staff. It is developed under the direction of the Joint Chiefs of Staff with support from the three military departments. Hitch has called this process prior to 1961 "essentially a pasting together of unilaterally developed service plans."[31] But the lack of unification or of an underlying principle was not as deleterious, he thought, as the fact that the planning was done in the void of military absolutism, that is, without relation to the realistic premises of "scarcity of resources" and "technological proliferation" with their demands for disciplined choices.

Effective March 1961 new planning procedures, categories, and terminology were established by civilian management: "all appropriate elements of the Defense Department in their respective areas of responsibility" were directed to participate.[32] First, the Joint Strategic Objectives Plan, carrying the recommendations of the Joint Chiefs of Staff across the entire range of defense missions, is submitted to the Secretary of Defense in the spring. It is based in part on "traditional" requirements studies, but increasingly it has reflected the impact of "military-economic" studies (that is, cost-effectiveness analyses) commissioned by the secretary and other civilian elements in the office of the Secretary of Defense. The secretary's review produces preliminary decisions which serve as "tentative force guidance" for the military in the makeup of the Five-Year Force Structure and Financial Program. Mr. McNamara's thinking on each area under review was set down in Draft Presidential Memoranda (DPM's), the drafting of which took place in the comptroller's office, specifically under the direction of his Deputy for Systems Analysis, Mr. Enthoven. However, in the case of research and development, the DPM issued from the Director of Defense Research and Engineering. The cost-effectiveness analyses, scheduled for completion in conjuction with the secretary's review, unquestionably were the largest factor in his decisions. They, not the JSOP, were the key tool in promoting the new way of looking at the defense problem. Hitch is explicit about this point: "I feel very strongly that whether one is choosing among particular items of equipment or among various policy proposals, it is extremely useful to array explicitly the alternatives and their respective costs and effectiveness. The procedures we are developing will promote this way of looking at defense problems, this way of deciding how best to defend the security of the United States."[33]

The next step is the vital bridging of the planning and budgeting phases. Hitch describes what he regarded as the most serious problem confronting civilian management. This was "to sort out all of the myriad programs and activities of the defense establishment and regroup them into meaningful program elements, i.e., integrated combinations of men, equipment and installations whose effectiveness could be *related to our national security objectives.*"[34] Working with other civilian elements and the military, the comptroller identified some one thousand "program elements." (The routing of "instructions" was to Assistant Secretaries for Financial Management at the service level.) These, in turn, would have to be grouped into a workable number of major programs or "program packages." This is a process of relating program elements to roles and missions, that is, assembling "related groups (or packages) of program elements that, for decision purposes, should be considered together because they support one another or because they were close substitutes . . . the unifying principle underlying each major program is a common mission or set of purposes for the elements involved."[35]

The program elements are "the basic building blocks" in the decision-making process. In the program data submitted to him, the comptroller requires that the full cost of each element be projected for five years (in the case of a new weapon system, eight years) and, moreover, that the costs be categorized as development, investment, or operating costs.

The comptroller's task is prodigious: he assembles and organizes the data submitted, combines elements into packages, conducts an almost continuous "program review"; in short, he is the point in the system "which brings together at one place and at one time all of the relevant information." It is clear that in the vital program review activity, the responsibility of the comptroller is not confined to a review of cost estimates. Because he has set the terms of discourse and because he occupies the focal point in the financial management system, his role in the "evaluational process" is a commanding one.

Programming is the middle phase between planning and budgeting. It dominates the overall process to the extent that it has been impossible to confine program review to the period between May and October, with the result that it overlaps the budget phase. It is the vital decision-making phase. The budget that follows, according to Secretary McNamara, is simply "the quantitative expression of the operating plan."[36] Actually the budget is the detailed costing of the first year or "increment" of the standing Five-Year Force Structure and Financial Program. Program change proposals, updating, and conversion of cost data to appropriation accounts are all part of the previous programming stage. The preparation and review of the budget constitute a process of working with approved programs to determine and display costs. The budget as a control or policy instrument is superseded by the prior function of programming.

Cost-Effectiveness Analyses

The new financial management system has had a direct and substantial impact on military planning processes. It has raised issues which go beyond questions of management to the very structure of civil-military relationships. A military participant in the Pentagon planning process has made the following observation on the McNamara impact:

Despite the many achievements of defense administration in the last three years, there is a serious weakness in its operation. It is the failure to develop a planning system to which both civil and military contribute according to their respective responsibilities and competencies. Military planners are concerned that *programming*, as it is now conceived by civilian authority, will dominate *the total defense planning process*, because that is where the weight of policy and organizational processes is brought to bear and where high level emphasis now lies . . . In effect, the military planning end of the bridge spanned by the Five Year Force Structure and Financing Program has been replaced by a body of ad hoc civilian sponsored, directed, or conducted studies and analyses to which the military contribution is largely facts and manpower operating under terms of reference established by civilian authority.[37]

The most significant ramification of the new management mode may well lie in the wrenching and straining it has produced. But it will have occurred at a point not contemplated by Mr. McNamara, that is, in the vital nexus of civilian and military professionalism.[38] If a new sense of professionalism had developed among career officers in the postwar era, a growing sensitivity about maintaining the integrity of that professionalism had also appeared in the decade of the 1960s. The reliance upon "military-economic studies," which are touted as the new mode of strategic planning, is seen as the gravest challenge to military professionalism. Such studies are understood as "civilian" studies falling in the military realm. Colonel Robert N. Ginsburgh points to the nub of the matter (from the perspective of a military professional): "It is not difficult for a military man to accept an adverse decision by his civilian superior based on nonmilitary considerations. It becomes extremely difficult, however, for him to reconcile himself to an adverse decision by his civilian superior based on *military* considerations."[39]

The military planner has lived with and accepted the highly political character of military planning. Referring to planning (at least in the past) as an "empirical and workable compromise" between such factors as "the perceived reality of danger, the nation's capability and willingness to pay, the pressure of special interests, and the collective judgments of many qualified and responsible men," Captain Stanley M. Barnes voices the objections of those who oppose an attempt to fit strategic planning into "a symmetrical and immaculate model of executive decision."[40] He leaves no doubt as to who has embarked on this mistaken enterprise:

> The men now in authority in the defense establishment are unquestionably as intelligent, dedicated, and aggressive as any who have undertaken this tremendous task. In a highly pragmatic political environment they are a composite of many disciplines. In the main, they are the social scientists concerned with the objectives and constraints governing the use of force as an instrument of policy, and the economist/systems analyst concerned with the more efficient planning and management of resources toward the ends of policy. As individuals, they had given a great deal of thought to defense issues before they arrived on the Washington scene. It is not unfair to say that they assumed their new responsibilities with preconceived ideas of what was wrong, why it was wrong, and what should be done to correct it.[41]

As Comptroller from 1949 to 1959, Wilfred J. McNeil did not think of "planning," "programming," and "budgeting" as discrete functions. However, as supervisor of the overall budgetary process, he developed an appreciation of the political character of planning which needs to be cited at some length as "civilian" support for the views of "military" commentators:

> Fortunately or unfortunately, the allocation cannot be entirely on a scientific basis. Allocations usually must be a matter of judgment . . . It is not simply a matter of figuring requirements and adding up their costs. The defense program must be judged in context with the Government program as a whole, and in the light of other desirable objectives, particularly in the fiscal and economic areas. This is the crux of the problem of budget planning at the national level. So while the Defense Department has a job to do, the amount of resources to be devoted to all Government functions and their allocation among those functions is a matter of subjective judgment . . . The test of the correctness

of these judgments is in how well the needs of the country have been met and how efficiently the Government managers have used the resources placed at their disposal. Neither of these tests is subject to any immediate or precise standard or measurement. This is an aspect of budgetary planning which often is not clearly understood. Many people, even though associated with the defense program for a long period of time, come to think of military requirements as finite quantities. This is a misconception. Virtually all military requirements stem from decisions on major force levels, and decisions on the levels of readiness of these forces. The determination of the forces required for national security and their level of readiness at any particular time is a complicated and by no means exact process. Decisions as to the course of research and development and weapons themselves, if rapid advances are to be made are, in part, a matter of judgment. There is a good deal of room for honest differences of judgment among equally competent persons. [42]

The military-economic studies or cost-effectiveness analyses which are a focal point of the growing sensitivity in civil-military relations are, by Mr. McNamara's admission, at the heart of the new mode of management. "When I say we are trying to establish a rational foundation for our military forces, I am thinking of exactly that kind of analysis," he has emphasized. [43] It is important, therefore, to underscore some of the more important aspects of cost-effectiveness analysis, and in doing so we shall note that it is inevitably a matter of contention even among civilian initiates. Something has been said already about the premises underlying cost-effectiveness studies, premises which constitute the environment within which the analyses are carried on. But it is not amiss to reiterate the dominating presence of the impinging factors ("scarcity of resources," "technological proliferation," and "active management at the top") in assessing the role of this management tool. Mr. Hitch and his deputy, Mr. Enthoven, have been the most articulate of the official advocates of cost-effectiveness analysis. In their efforts at explanation and persuasion they have, no doubt, often hurt their own case through necessary oversimplification. Yet, in contrast with the discussions of cost-effectiveness analysis and systems analysis in academic circles, the positions taken by Hitch and Enthoven suggest a defensiveness that does not aid an already aggravated situation.

The Hitch-Enthoven argument is that the "real objective" of military planning, and therefore the explanation for the introduction of cost-effectiveness analyses, is "to use our resources as best we can." At the same time an all but unlimited substitution of means to satisfy wants is available (making dollars, in most cases, a satisfactory term of measurement). The unavoidable conclusion is that choosing weapons *and strategies* is in important respects an economic problem, a problem of disciplined choice under an economic criterion. Moreover, and this is understood as sealing the argument, this way of looking at the defense problem allows for the necessary data to be portrayed for "top management" in such a way as to make "meaningful decisions" the end result. Cost-effectiveness analyses, in a word, are no more than an efficient tool of the new management. A lack of candor about the assumptions, implicit and explicit, characterizes this argument. In their concern that others have not been able to follow the "inexorable logic" of cost effectiveness, the proponents exhibit a blind side. There has seldom been criticism that cost-effectiveness analysts have worked from their own assumptions to conclusions in an invalid manner; the basic issue is the validity of the assumptions themselves, and the degree to which they are subjected to analysis.[44]

Perhaps the strongest case for "military systems analysis" has been made by E. S. Quade of the RAND Corporation; at the same time no one has made a more searching critique.[45] Quade poses the primary problem for the cost-effectiveness analyst. He "is likely to be forced to deal with problems in which the difficulty lies in deciding *what ought to be done, not simply in how to do it.* In such a situation, far more attention must be devoted to establishing objectives, criteria, and alternatives. The total analysis is thus a more complex and less neat and tidy procedure which is seldom suitable for a quantitative optimization over the whole problem."[46] If the analyst recognizes that he is working within the framework of "a given budget" or "a given desired level of military effectiveness," it must also be recognized that such "givens" pose the prior and larger questions. This is the not easy problem of finding agreement on a working basis for objectives and criteria. Quade underlines the relative importance of choosing "the right objective" (goal) over choosing "the right alternative" (system or strategy): "Great attention must be paid to initial conditions; that is, to the assumptions which limit the problem and set the background against which the initial attempt at a solution is to be made. The situation is not like that of an *empirical science*, which starts with observed facts, but more like that of *mathematics*, where the results take any 'validity' they might have in the real world *from the assumptions* ... it is important that the assumptions be the 'right' assumptions."[47] Captain Barnes raised the question whether there were any explicit military assumptions underlying the McNamara-Hitch system:

The key element of all analyses is the use of assumptions. The key assumptions, which can swing results one way or another, have a way of being removed from conclusions to such distances that their criticality is forgotten. They are frequently military in character, and there is always the question as to who is responsible for their validity. The assumptions which are implicit or explicit in the total of the major decisions reached in the last three years, in effect constitute a national strategic appraisal and concept governing the whole defense posture. These premises do not now exist as such in any coherent form. Their present formlessness can lead to both inconsistency and rigidity—the comfortable assumption, for example, that our enemies will be as rational and logical as we like to think we are ... The question of assumptions highlights an even larger problem. Military concepts of problem solving are much more than logical process alone. In the same way that systems analysis has a major contribution to make to problem solving, military concepts of accountability should influence decision making. The basic precept of military professionalism is accountability for some part of national security.

Operationally this is direct and inescapable. In other matters, it takes the form of service reputation for professionalism, and its consequences are highly effective constraints. In evaluating the defense planning organization, the first question should be—where, short of the highest levels, does accountability commensurate with authority, restrain incompetence, arrogance, and all other human frailties which can inhibit responsible and objective performance of duty? [48]

The point of this criticism is that in the determination of objectives, in establishing working assumptions, the dramatis personnae become the critical element. Setting the goals of military planning, within a framework of overall national political goals, is central to military professionalism; providing a series of alternative means for the achievement of military goals is also central to military professionalism. There is no scientific basis for supposing that the civilian analyst has superior or even comparable credentials for such tasks. Yet, insofar as the premises and the terms of the defense discourse are set by "top management," as they have been since 1961, the role of the analyst threatens a severe derangement of the civil-military structure. The goal of "pluralist planning," if it can be established as a goal, required at the minimum "professional pluralism."

Quade gives short shrift to the contention that cost-effectiveness analyses are simply a management tool or that they are "neutral." Indeed, it is "primarily to recommend" policy that such studies are undertaken in the first place; they are "attempts to influence policy." In a cryptic piece of advice to analysts, Quade suggests "first, find out what to recommend, and second, make these recommendations convincing!" While Enthoven, particularly, has laid stress on the application of "the scientific method" to problems of economic choice, Quade argues that "it is by no means clear that there is any unique method which can be termed scientific." [49] Warning against solutions which have been "simplified and reduced to mathematical form by a drastic idealization and aggregation of the real world factors," he points to the sharply limited utility of analysis: "Analysis is sufficient to reach a policy conclusion only when the objectives are agreed upon by the policy makers. In defense policy in particular . . . objectives are not, in fact, agreed upon . . . hence, nonanalytical methods must be used for a final reconciliation of views." [50] Ultimately, of course, the "judgment" applied by the decision-maker will determine the impact of cost-effectiveness analyses. Robert S. McNamara stands as the first of its proponents.

Civilians and Military

Secretary McNamara made his major impact on defense decision-making through the new mode of management discussed above. This served, in his mind, to make extensive reorganization of the department unnecessary. Yet there have been important organizational developments at the "Defense" level which reflect a firmly held tenet of the secretary's management philosophy, that is, the "single-manager" concept. The first of the defense agencies, the Defense Atomic Support Agency (DASA) and the Defense Communications Agency (DCA), were established in 1959. They are in the command line in support of activities of the Joint Chiefs of Staff; consequently, they report to the Secretary of Defense "through the Joint Chiefs of Staff." Mr. McNamara established the Defense Intelligence Agency (DIA) by directive in 1961, and this became the third defense agency to report "through the Joint Chiefs of Staff." In addition, he established two other defense agencies which, because of the "nonmilitary" character of their activities, report directly to the Secretary of Defense: The Defense Supply Agency (DSA) was created by directive in 1961, and the Defense Contract Audit Agency (DCAA) in 1965. The objective was to put under single management common supplies and services in the one case, and the auditing function in the other. DCAA also has the purpose of separating auditors from the services whose contracts are being audited; it was hoped that the agency might expedite a change from cost-plus-fixed-fee contracting to lowest-bidder contracting.

Secretaries McElroy and Gates had little trouble in setting up DASA and DCA, but a single intelligence agency at the defense level inevitably evoked reaction. Secretary McNamara's justification for DIA had a strong management flavor: he stressed "unity of effort," "a more efficient allocation of intelligence resources," and "more effective management of . . . intelligence activities." McNamara summed up: "It is to avoid . . . duplication and eliminate . . . overlapping that we are proposing to establish this control agency."[51] He conceded there were "divergent views" whether a more effective intelligence capacity, in addition to management gains, would be a product of the new agency, but he insisted that in the "long run" this, too, would be the result. He told Congress that the "capability within the individual services for preparing detailed intelligence reports has, of course, been transferred to DIA," and that the services themselves would not have representatives on the U.S. Intelligence Board.[52] The consolidation of technical activities represented by DASA, DSA, and DCAA has been inevitable and desirable. On the other hand, the establishment of a "single," defense-wide, intelligence agency poses in microcosm many of the problems which have beset a "single" Department of Defense. What is the value of pluralism and competition in the interrelated areas of policy, strategy, plans, and operations as opposed to the value of consolidation and economy? As answers to such questions are more the result of "judgment" than of analytical techniques, the answers are not obvious.

Mr. McNamara saw the organization of the office of the Secretary of Defense (OSD) itself as a problem of the most efficient management of the overall military establishment. There was no longer any question after the Reorganization Act of 1958 about division of functions between OSD and the services. It would depend entirely on the Secretary of

Defense how far he would bring the day-to-day operations of the military establishment to the "Defense" level. Inasmuch as the "support line" and the "command line" both ran to the Secretary of Defense, Mr. McNamara felt he could be most effective and exert the greatest initiative by exercising direct supervision and control over all "functions." There was a clear equation in his mind between functional monopoly and the "direction, authority, and control" of the Secretary of Defense. This would also mean fewer, rather than more, individuals reporting directly to the Secretary of Defense. His first steps were to put four task forces to work on major functional areas as a means of initiating the new financial management system, and to set up an office of Organizational and Management Planning Studies in the office of the General Counsel. The task forces were ad hoc devices and were not employed again. They aroused immediate criticism because of the fact that Mr. McNamara was inclined to keep their membership and their recommendations secret. The fact that the task force "commanders" were known suggested to some that "novices" were meddling in matters beyond their ken.[53] This would be the beginning (in the McNamara era) of a continuing controversy over the "civilianization" of the Defense Department.

The Secretary of Defense is authorized under the National Security Act to carry seven positions in OSD at the assistant secretary level. The manner in which Mr. McNamara experimented with the distribution of authority and functions among his closest subordinates is revealed in the pattern of assistant secretary appointments. The seven assistant secretaries in 1966 were: (1) Comptroller, (2) Systems Analysis, (3) International Security Affairs, (4) Installations and Logistics, (5) Manpower and Personnel, (6) Administration, and (7) Public Affairs. We have already noted that while Mr. Hitch was comptroller he was undoubtedly the most important member of the McNamara group. On Hitch's retirement, Mr. McNamara in effect put two assistant secretaries in the planning-programming-budgeting process, namely, Robert N. Anthony as comptroller and Alain B. Enthoven for Systems Analysis. The new prominence of Mr. Enthoven came at some cost to the office of the Director of Defense Research and Engineering.[54] What has been surprising, and in some quarters disappointing, is the decline of DDR&E since 1961. During the McNamara tenure, the director, who stands above the assistant secretary level (along with the General Counsel), was not the independent and significant source of influence on the Secretary of Defense that was contemplated in 1958. This directorate has been occupied from the beginning by the "Livermore Group." The first of three occupants, Herbert York, left the Pentagon in April 1961 after a three-year term. Mr. McNamara's first appointee, Harold Brown, held the office until October 1965, when he was succeeded by John S. Foster, Jr. If there ever was a "Livermore position" on weapons development, once it was transplanted from California to Washington it tended to merge with that of Robert S. McNamara. A vast transcript of *public* testimony displays a startling identity of viewpoint on "strategy, technology, and economy" between Harold Brown and the Secretary of Defense. This harmony would explain in part Brown's next assignment as Secretary of the Air Force.

Solis Horwitz served as "management counsel" from the outset. His office of Organizational and Management Planning Studies, placed first in the office of General Counsel, was subsequently given independent status. Finally, Horwitz, who was also acting as coordinator of the National Communications System, was elevated to Assistant Secretary of Defense for Administration. Thomas D. Morris, serving as Assistant Secretary of Defense for Installations and Logistics and later in the Manpower and Personnel billet, was another major source of support rather than influence. The late John T. McNaughton was an important intellectual backstop for the secretary, first as General Counsel and subsequently as Assistant Secretary of Defense for International Security

Affairs. Mr. McNamara was not hesitant to move his most valued subordinates from one position to another. The most striking example of this brings the post-1958 relationship between the Secretary of Defense and the service secretaries into sharp focus.

It has been necessary since 1958, and particularly since 1961, for a man serving as civilian head of one of the three military departments to fully grasp the extent to which his office has changed. It is a large order and has not always occurred (more than a dozen men occupied the three service secretaryships under McNamara). To cope with the problem of the assimilation of service secretaries, Mr. McNamara did not hesitate to detail men from OSD to each of the services. Cyrus R. Vance was sent down from the office of General Counsel to be Secretary of the Army after Elvis Stahr discovered a "once-in-a-lifetime" opportunity at Indiana University.[55] After first working with John Connally and Fred Korth, Mr. McNamara had Paul Nitze, Assistant Secretary of Defense for International Security Affairs, assigned to the Secretary of the Navy post. And Harold Brown, Director of Defense Research and Engineering for more than four years, was appointed Secretary of the Air Force after Eugene M. Zuckert resigned in September 1965. Mr. Zuckert, who felt that many of Stahr's criticisms were well taken, took note of the changed role of the service secretary upon his retirement. Approaching an evaluation of the service secretary's role "with concern, if not detachment," he felt that while Mr. McNamara had removed the service secretary from "operations" and confined him to "resources," two areas of significance were still open to him. The service secretary, first of all, was "the man in the middle": "I had hoped the President would accept the fine point that, if I was to be effective in my job, I had to act and to be regarded by Air Force people as an advocate of their basic programs . . . I doubt that President Kennedy accepted this view. He wanted my support, and while he was willing . . . to stand for a certain amount of 'independent' thinking, that independence must in the future be neither frequent nor important." Second, the vast military establishment "simply cannot be managed efficiently from one central point": "I am convinced that this responsibility must be parceled out. The military services, essentially organized around the medium in which each one operates, offer through the Service Secretaries precisely that middle level of management which cannot be discharged as well anywhere else in the Department of Defense."[56] Vance, incidentally, had to be recalled from his Army post when Roswell L. Gilpatric resigned as Deputy Secretary of Defense in January 1964. Mr. McNamara has paid his own homage to "the-man-rather-than-the-office" notion.

Secretary McNamara opined in the spring of 1961 that relationships between himself and the Joint Chiefs of Staff were "closer than they have ever been before between Secretaries and the Chiefs."[57] Three years later, responding to criticisms about his relationships with the JCS, Mr. McNamara cited statements from former JCS Chairmen, Generals Lyman Lemnitzer and Maxwell Taylor, that they were "satisfactory."[58] Interestingly, one of the issues about Mr. McNamara's relationships with the military is the existence of the issue itself. The Secretary of Defense has been steadfast in his denial of anything untoward between him and the Chiefs. He asserts that he brought about "a major change" in the planning role of the JCS without, apparently, recognizing this as a possible basis for concern by the Chiefs. Typically, he will point out as he did in 1964: "I think the Chiefs have calculated that they have considered the fiscal 1965 budget and associated matters *on 104 occasions* in order to form a basis for their recommendations to me . . . never have the views of the senior military officials been solicited *as frequently,* nor considered as carefully." But after noting the volume of traffic between the secretary and the Joint Chiefs of Staff, Mr. McNamara adds the following: "never has there been as little hesitation to overrule the recommendations of a particular service when that service's recommendations *appeared to be directed to the parochial interest of the service rather than to the national interest.* It is this latter condition which sometimes leads to controversy."[59] On more than one occasion Mr. McNamara contemplated the provision of the National Security Act which reads: "After first informing the Secretary of Defense, a member of the Joint Chiefs of Staff may make such recommendations to Congress relating to the Department of Defense as he may consider appropriate."[60] Although granting that it was "very clear," the secretary at first thought this "a rather unusual provision of the law." He was prepared to live with it; yet on the other hand he felt there was "no need for" a Chief to appeal directly to the President since he, the Secretary of Defense, would have presented "a balanced view" to the Commander in Chief earlier. By way of implementing the provision, Mr. McNamara provided guidance for the Chiefs in their Congressional appearances in a memorandum over the signature of Deputy Secretary Vance, dated January 11, 1965.[61] If pressed for his personal opinion (Mr. McNamara thinks "asked" would, indeed, be better terminology), a Chief must first indicate whether he has expressed his views to "appropriate authorities" in the Department of Defense; then he must indicate that, notwithstanding his personal views, he abides by "the departmental position"; finally, he may state his own view so long as he also advances the considerations which support the departmental position. In short, the Chief is compelled to give what Mr. McNamara calls "a balanced view," rather than advocacy of his own position. Asked by Senator Richard Russell of Georgia if this guidance did not run counter to the intent of the statute, Mr. McNamara insisted that "that is the way I want people to present recommendations to me, and I assume you would likewise."[62] Senator Russell made it sufficiently clear that the time-honored adversary system was adequate for the purposes of the Senate. The concern of Russell, Chairman of the

Senate Armed Services Committee, was similar to that expressed by John G. Norris of the *Washington Post* when he wrote of General Curtis E. LeMay that "not many Pentagon leaders, concerned with their future, reply so fully and frankly when asked for their professional views which differ with those of the Administration."[63]

The Army had sole occupancy of the chairmanship of the Joint Chiefs of Staff during Mr. McNamara's tenure. General Nathan F. Twining's term as Chairman was to extend to August 1961; however, General Lyman L. Lemnitzer was appointed Chairman in October 1960. Lemnitzer became Army Chief of Staff in 1959 after the resignation of General Maxwell Taylor; his term as Chairman would be short-lived also. General Taylor, who had been occupying a post in the White House as special military advisor to the President, became Chairman of the Joint Chiefs of Staff after the unhappiness of the Bay of Pigs in October 1961. General Earle G. Wheeler succeeded Taylor in 1964.[64] In the summer of 1961, General Curtis E. LeMay relieved General Thomas D. White as Air Force Chief of Staff. White, who had served a four-year term, was able, articulate, and of a theoretical cast of mind. LeMay was tough, practical, and relied heavily on a long "experience" in strategic air warfare. Three years later Mr. McNamara clearly wished to remove him, but President Johnson extended LeMay's term seven months to permit him to complete a thirty-five-year career. Admiral George W. Anderson, Jr., succeeded Admiral Arleigh Burke as Chief of Naval Operations in 1961 as Burke finished an unprecedented six years on the Joint Chiefs of Staff. Anderson was appointed Ambassador to Portugal in August 1963 after two short years with Mr. McNamara. Admiral David L. McDonald thereupon became Chief of Naval Operations. The continuity in office of both service secretaries and members of the JCS does not match that of the 1957-1961 period as much as Mr. McNamara sought to achieve a comparable record. A brief discussion of the "Anderson Affair" illustrates something of Mr.

McNamara's expectations about the relationship which should obtain between the Chiefs and the Secretary of Defense.

On April 5, 1963, Admiral Anderson appeared before the McClellan Subcommittee conducting the "TFX Contract Investigation" and presented testimony which the chairman thought possibly the finest the committee had received.[65] The testimony gave evidence that much more than the TFX occupied the mind of the Chief of Naval Operations. Anderson felt compelled to state that he deplored any speculation that the military were challenging "the necessary and proper American tradition of civilian control," and (at another point) that he, personally, was not doing so in his testimony.[66] He emphasized his responsibility as Chief of Naval Operations to provide "the best" weapons possible and to see that men under his command be provided "the greatest margin of safety consistent with the hazardous tasks they perform." Anderson observed that he had had two nephews killed in naval aviation and had a son serving as a Navy test pilot.

Turning to the question of procuring the TFX for the Navy, Admiral Anderson put heavy stress on "an edge of advantage" in the performance of a system: "Those of us who have learned the hard way of the importance of this edge attach great significance to what might otherwise appear inconsequential differences between two competing pieces of military hardware. I know of no way to attach numbers, weight, or scores to such intangibles."[67] The Navy did not consider that a combined development project for both the Navy and the Air Force was technically feasible, but accepted a contrary directive from the Secretary of Defense "in consonance with the military tradition of carrying out orders." Thereafter, the Navy recommended that the design submitted by Boeing would best meet the needs of both services. Again, an adverse decision from the Secretary of Defense resulted in "full cooperation" from the Navy, Anderson insisted.

However, in retrospect, he felt that he had probably not communicated sufficiently to higher authority the degree to which the Navy had made "compromises" to keep the program viable. "I am sure that we have all learned a lesson in this case," Admiral Anderson concluded; "this experience has taught me to talk it back and forth and try to hammer out the differences of view or the evaulation of independent judgments. This has also taught me a lesson, to perhaps to be more contentious in matters in the future." [68]

One month later in an address to the Navy League in San Juan, Admiral Anderson was underscoring "mutual confidence" and "mutual respect" between civilian and military leadership. [69] His emphasis on the values which were the very fiber of relationships among military men carried an obvious point; he was concerned that the new civilian leadership in the Department of Defense did not seem to understand or share those values. An answer was forthcoming the following month. Mr. Enthoven's address to the Naval War College in June 1963 indicated a "value gap" between significant segments of the civilian and military leadership. [70] In August, Admiral Anderson failed to obtain the normal reappointment after two years. He summed up his views in a dramatic appearance before the National Press Club on September 4: "I should like to express my views on certain aspects of the Department of Defense at this time. These views, if given due consideration, might be a factor in insuring that our country indeed will have the necessary military strength, the best strategy, and the finest military leadership. There are some tendencies which give me great concern . . . if [they] . . . are checked and redirected now, the Defense Department will move forward to a better position than ever in its history." [71] Anderson pointed to five tendencies in all which concerned him. Most important, he felt, was a lack of confidence and trust between the civilian and military echelons in the Department of Defense. "Mutual confidence and trust are built the hard way," he contended, "and can be broken down

quickly by one or two impulsive actions or intemperate judgments." The critical area in this instance was weapons selection. "I am concerned," Anderson continued, "that . . . there
may not be a full appreciation of the decisiveness of a narrow
edge of performance, both to achieve maximum safety, and
to succeed in combat." Responding directly to Enthoven, he
indicated that service experience was being subordinated to
the evaluations of "analysts": "we feel emotionally aroused
as·well as dispassionately concerned if the recommendations
of the uniformed chiefs of our services, each backed up by
competent military and civilian professional staffs, are altered
or overruled without interim consultation, explanation and
discussion."[72] Anderson continued by pointing to a specific
difficulty: "the operations analyst—properly concerned with
'cost effectiveness'—seems to be working at the wrong
echelon—above the professional military level rather than in
an advisory capacity to the military who should thoroughly
appreciate this assistance. Specialists cannot, without danger,
extrapolate their judgments into fields in which they do not
have expert knowledge. Unfortunately, today in the Pentagon an unhealthy imbalance has resulted because at times
specialists are used as experts in areas outside their fields."[73]
In concluding, he took note of the role of the Joint Chiefs of
Staff. Never should they become "merely a rubber stamp to
the Secretary of Defense." "As a collective body, the Chiefs
must represent military requirements from differing viewpoints, so that we do not ignore the value of mixed, balanced, diversified forces." Nor should the full force of JCS
recommendations to the President and Congress be "dulled in
any way in transmission."[74]

The traditional posture of Admiral Anderson was incom-
patible with the new posture of Secretary McNamara. Both
parties seemed anxious to make the point. The episode, however, does raise a significant question about the character of
civil-military relations during Mr. McNamara's tenure. Jack
Raymond of the *New York Times,* whose vantage point for

observing the American military establishment over the years must be considered excellent, writes that Secretary McNamara has been accused "accurately" of forcing the armed services to "speak with one voice" and of "overriding the voice of professional military experience."[75] Raymond fears that McNamara does not recognize that "the unique American-style open political warfare indulged in by the military in advocating certain national security goals has served to provide an 'outlet for frustrations which, in other settings, has been the catalyst to set off an outburst of militarism.' The American style, in which military officers are encouraged to speak out even on subjects that are not directly related to their professional responsibilities, has served also to identify them publicly with recognizable political attitudes even when these bear no party label. This has made covert adventurism on the part of the military a rather difficult prospect."[76]

In our survey of the period preceding 1961 we found it useful to formulate two sets of precedents for the eighth Secretary of Defense. However, the experience of 1961-68 does not fit within the outlines of either the generalist or the functionalist role. Mr. McNamara's tenure provides a new precedent and therefore a new base point from which to assess the role of the Secretary of Defense and its present direction. The functionary whose special competence is management and who seeks to bring each separate operation in the organization under his purview is seen in the Department of Defense in the Eisenhower years. The functionalist concept is the concept of the manager carried to the point where the manager participates directly in each functional activity of the organization. With the credentials of manager and in the name of efficiency, the Eisenhower-Rockefeller Secretary of Defense undertakes to carry out policy which he has not had any major role in formulating. Indeed, policy is the preserve of the political and military professionals; the secretary will convey policy to the organization and translate it into effective programs. This conception of the role of the Secretary of

Defense is the converse of the generalist concept. The latter puts policy at the heart of the secretarial role. Because policy is central, the secretary is not a functionary but, in the supreme sense of the term, a politician. The Forrestal-Lovett-Gates Secretary of Defense relies on political prudence; that is to say, he accepts bargaining and negotiating with various sources in an effort to establish the broad outlines of policy. The rationality of techniques and exclusive processes is confined to subordinate levels.

The McNamara experience represents an attempt to fuse in the secretarial role the two concepts, one based on policy and the other on the managerial function. The McNamara fusion fails because it does not extend to policy and prudence the primacy of position they must have. The secretarial role that is the result of the premises and the activity of Mr. McNamara establishes the primacy of technical process. Policy is understood as a derivative of technical process and technical rationality, and consequently as a function of the manager. In this respect, the McNamara role differs as radically from the functionalist concept as it does from the generalist concept. The former was distinctive in its preoccupation with management; the latter was unique in its focus on policy. It may be granted that the Secretary of Defense role is necessarily bi-modal, that it cannot be characterized by a singular regard for either policy or management. What is at issue in the evolution of the role of the Secretary of Defense is more fundamental. In the search for a more adequate role formulation, the premises of the generalist concept cannot be arrayed against the premises of the functionalist concept, nor can the former be made an appendage of the latter as in the McNamara fusion. The premises of the generalist concept must set the structure and quality of the secretarial role, giving direction and purpose to the management function. The strengths of the functionalist role are such as to reenforce and support policy; they are incapable of establishing anything but a caricature of policy.

Secretary McNamara's exercise of "direction, authority,

and control" in the Department of Defense has been an effort to encompass within his purview the full decision spectrum. It is a supreme effort to bring the policy, strategy, resources, and operations continuum within the terms of an a priori system. Mr. McNamara has consciously undertaken to elaborate and impose system. At the center of this effort is a rejection of political process which alone can be productive of policy. The establishment of technical process is the result, in part, of the clarity and sophistication of method which it provides as opposed to the more roughly hewn categories of political process. There is little doubt that the restoration of policy to primacy will depend in some measure on greater theoretical articulation of the criteria of politics.[77] But the issue of the role of the Secretary of Defense is far graver. Mr. McNamara can be forgiven for shortness in rejecting charges that the Pentagon is "run by computers." He understands fully as well as Secretary Forrestal that "It is the men." The Forrestal-Lovett-Gates understanding of the secretarial role rests on unassailable ground; but the ground cannot go unmanned. What it required for its defense is the presence of political men. If political men do not command the heights, lesser men than the new technocrats will some day play the role of usurper.[78]

Two case studies of the new management follow. In the next two chapters we shall note the manner in which Mr. McNamara confronted the interrelated problems of strategy, technology, and weapons selection. His "decisions" on a follow-on manned bomber and a second nuclear carrier reveal themselves as significant tests of the premises and tools of the new management. They are, at the same time, tests of the viability of civil-military relationships in an era of change.

3
A Manned Bomber

 The Joint Strategic Objectives Plan (1968-1975), submitted to the Secretary of Defense by the Joint Chiefs of Staff in March 1966, recommended full-scale development of an advanced manned strategic aircraft (AMSA) with an initial operational capability (IOC) in fiscal year 1974. AMSA would succeed the last two series (G and H) of the B-52, the production of which was closed down in 1962. The eight-engined jet bomber had been the mainstay of the Strategic Air Command's nuclear delivery capability since 1956. On June 14, 1966, Congressman L. Mendel Rivers of South Carolina, volatile successor of Carl Vinson as Chairman of the House Armed Services Committee, speaking on the floor of the House said, "So help me God, we are going to have a follow-on bomber if it kills everyone in the Department of Defense, and I die in the process."[1] Secretary of Defense Robert S. McNamara rejected the recommendation of the Joint Chiefs of Staff, as well as the prediction of Congressman Rivers, just as he had rejected every other effort to begin full-scale development of a follow-on manned bomber for the previous five years.

Basically attuned to the weapons technology race between the United States and the Soviet Union, Secretary McNamara was governed by two major considerations in addressing the problem of general nuclear war. He was convinced, first, that the technology of the 1960s would remain more or less stable and provided more than enough "choices" in weapons and strategy. He was convinced, second, that the enormity of nuclear arms was outside the grasp of laymen; consequently, steps toward "minimization of risk" were urgent. The AMSA decision is an excellent focal point for a study of Mr. McNamara's approach to choices of strategy and choices of weapons. The interrelationship of such choices is apparent; what is more striking is the relationship of the intellectual mode of the Secretary of Defense and the choices that have been made.

A Technological Plateau

The French military theoretician General André Beaufre has reminded contemporary students of the "defense problem" that some of the conventional wisdom of his profession has not lost its place in a scientific age. In a short, classic study, Beaufre takes note of developments in the United States: "the importance of defense problems is obvious and, primarily in America, a growing number of analysts are devoting themselves to the question and trying to assemble that fund of learning which must be the basis of progress. But in this slow, painful advance made by the social sciences the guiding principle, a philosophy, and the operational concept, which means strategy, are missing."[2] Strategy, he notes, "like our civilization, is being carried along by the galloping advance of science." What has most characterized the thought of contemporary students is the confusion of strategy with logistics and tactics—an inevitable result of the attempt to render strategy scientific.

> The thought processes applicable to tactics or logistics are almost entirely methodistic, their object being the rational employment of the military resources available in order to produce a given result . . . strategic thinking, however, is a mental process, at once abstract and rational, which must be capable of synthesizing both

psychological and material data. The strategist must have a great
capacity *both* for analysis and for synthesis; analysis is necessary
to assemble the data on which he makes his diagnosis, synthesis in
order to produce from these data the diagnosis itself—and the
diagnosis in fact amounts to a choice between alternative courses
of action.[3]

Both tactics and logistics smack of material science such as
engineering, with stress on the interplay of material factors,
Beaufre contends. But in strategy, as in all human affairs, "it
is ideas which must be the dominant and guiding
force . . . strategy must be a continuous process of original
thinking, based upon hypotheses which must be proved true
or false as action proceeds." The process of science proceeding methodistically from set propositions is rule out in strategic thought by Beaufre. Strategy "must work on hypotheses and produce solutions by truly original thought . . . it
must rely on imagination and be the fruit of meditation . . .
there can be no rules for the inventive ability required."
Most especially strategy must discard "rigid and dangerous hypotheses like some recent theories, most of American origin, which are based on a mathematical evaluation of
probabilities. Instead it must be based on a whole gamut of
possibilities." [4]

Thus defined, strategic thought was not a congenial process for the mind of Robert McNamara. There was nothing in
his previous experience, of course, to provide him with a
grasp of high strategy and international political-military relations. Moreover, Mr. McNamara gathered around him in
1961 men who did not complement his own intellectual processes so much as reenforce them. In Beaufre's terms, "logistic thought" was the mode of the new management. Within
this frame the strategic problem was understood as one of
maximizing the possibilities inherent in the enormous postwar technological spasm which, however, would appear to
have run its course. Moreover, a logistic strategy of technological exploitation, as opposed to a more dynamic strategy

of acceleration, would not be provocative in character and, at the same time would itself contribute to minimization of risk. If Mr. McNamara's approach to strategy in logistic terms was more or less inevitable, so too, no doubt, was his choice of a "conservative" logistic strategy. This choice is explained only in part by the rapid pace of obsolescence and the cost of weapons. More fundamental was the secretary's basic understanding of the character of the arms race. There was, to begin with, his tendency to cast the problem in terms of quantifiables—to see the arms race in essentially quantitative terms—but underlying that was his conviction that a relative stability characterized weapons technology in the 1960s. The argument that the arms race, on the contrary, has a dynamic, qualitative character did not appear to carry weight.[5] The "conservatism" of the military which causes them to put a premium on flexibility, hedges, safety factors, and so forth is at bottom a "dynamic" point of view and thus puts them at the opposite pole from the logistic conservatism of Secretary McNamara.

The issues involved in the concept of a "technological plateau" and Mr. McNamara's appreciation of the arms race have been amply discussed. After his retirement as Head of the Office of Science and Technology under President Kennedy and President Johnson, Jerome B. Wiesner joined with Herbert F. York, first Director of Defense Research and Engineering, to contend that the security of the United States had diminished rather than increased as a result of an enhanced military posture.[6] While Mr. McNamara, perhaps, could not be expected to concur in that particular formulation, Wiesner and York did emphasize a theme in which the secretary did concur. They stressed that "technoligical surprise" is not a threat to national security and that major breakthroughs are not to be expected. Technological efforts to establish a defense against missile-delivered nuclear weapons were implausible, if not altogether futile. This was paired with the interesting contention that such efforts, moreover, were provocative–they merely spurred offense technology on to greater gains. This is not so much an argument of technological stability as it is one of a technological dead end on the defense side and technological deacceleration on the offense side. Extreme in its formulation, the Wiesner-York argument, nonetheless, reflected much of the thought of the civilian management of the Department of Defense during the McNamara tenure.

The argument was quickly countered, however, by outsiders who had close connections with the Department of Defense. Eugene Wigner, Director of the classified National Academy of Sciences "Project Harbor" study on civil defense, took sharp exception to the views of Wiesner and York. Wigner explicitly rejected the contention that "on any scale of investment, the combination of larger numbers and smaller size results in greater effectiveness of the missile system." (The argument, incidentally, is an ideal example of the "logistic approach.") James R. Schlesinger, in a review of Wiesner's book, *Where Science and Politics Meet* (New York, 1965), which includes the October 1964 article Wiesner co-authored with York ("National Security and the Nuclear Test Ban"), states that Wiesner "resisted efforts to preserve the strategic superiority of the United States or to push ahead with programs for civil or ballistic-missile defense." Schlesinger points up what he calls the "underlying theology" of the Wiesnerian viewpoint. There are three dogmas: (1) "Self-reenforcing mutual suspicion has led to a violent and accelerating arms race"; (2) "It is the joint interest of both sides that they cease augmenting the weapons stock"; and (3) "Proposals put forward 'in good faith' are rejected by both sides because of a negative state of mind born of fear." As a dissenter, Schlesinger notes that there might be some basis for such mistrust on our part to proposals put forward by the Soviets, and that "utopian optimism born of hope" might prove even more detrimental than "a negative state of mind born of fear." He concludes that "Dr. Wiesner's handling of the state of military technology can be interpreted only in terms of wishful thinking."[7]

One of the best indications of Mr. McNamara's attitude is found in connection with the Nuclear Test Ban Treaty hearings, during which he directed himself to an appraisal of the existing technological and military capabilities of the United States and the Soviet Union. Typically, the secretary stressed that the total number of nuclear warheads in the U.S. inventory was in the tens of thousands. This factor more than any other seemed to suggest to him that the treaty posed no threat to the strategic superiority of the United States. Turning to the criterion for comparing technological capabilities (concerning which we have the most information), namely, yield-to-weight ratios, Mr. McNamara stated: "the Soviet Union appears to be technologically more advanced than we are in the high yield range, that is to say, in the tens of megatons; below that yield, the relative capability shifts progressively in favor of the United States . . . The apparent Soviet technological advantage at the upper end of the yield spectrum has resulted from a considered decision by the United States not to concentrate efforts in this field."[8] Mr. McNamara's reasons for this considered decision are numerous but of a piece. Preoccupied with the problem of missile penetration of *projected,* elaborate Soviet defenses (the Secretary of Defense at no time felt that the Soviet Union possessed an effective, operational ABM capability), Mr. McNamara put a premium on the development of low- and middle-range yield warheads deployed in large numbers of MINUTE-MAN and POLARIS missiles to assure penetration by saturation. He had a much higher confidence in "killing" military targets with "two or three smaller weapons instead of one very large one." And, inevitably, the secretary has argued that "for a given resource input we achieve higher target destruction with our smaller systems."

Mr. McNamara testified that the "prolongation of our

technological superiority will be a principal direct military effect" of the Nuclear Test Ban Treaty and that by "limiting Soviet testing to the underground environment . . . where the United States has substantially more experience, we can at least retard Soviet progress." That the Soviets would be confined to an environment in which they could pursue their most needed testing did not alter the judgment of the Secretary of Defense. The United States had not tested missile-site survivability with high-yield, near-surface bursts sufficiently to remove "uncertainties," but those uncertainties, Mr. McNamara contended, could be "measured and taken account of." It was also true that confinement to the underground environment would remove the possibility of an "optimum design" for warheads; however, a "satisfactory design" would still be possible.

Mr. McNamara's "logistic strategy" requires that in the process of pursuing a particular technological opportunity the specific operational requirements and the cost effectiveness of a weapon system be confirmed before full-scale development, production, and deployment are authorized. The weapon must fulfill a "military requirement" defined and approved years in advance of operation, and the potential operational benefit must be worth the cost projected in cost-effectiveness analyses. The reaction to these constraints has not resulted in a fruitful dialogue between defense management and its critics. It is fair to say that the point of the criticism is not as Mr. Hitch has portrayed it. The widespread fear is not that the department is bent on building the cheapest weapon, but that its procedures will "abort" the full gestation of ideas and hardware. Klaus Knorr and Oskar Morgenstern, whose standing is such that they may have legitimized criticism by a recent study, have asked "whether the recent emphasis on cost-effectiveness may not be too much of a good thing," and whether "the rather ill-defined military requirement approach to authorizing an inventive effort does not constitute an excessive restraint." They note that:

cost-effectiveness studies can obviously be valuable when one compares military systems with other systems producing similar specific outputs and manifesting a similar sensitivity to important environmental conditions—although even here various uncertainties may cause such studies to run the risk of a misleading dependence on pseudo-accuracy. In particular, the derivation of the numbers in terms of which "effectiveness" is measured is itself a far more delicate procedure than these studies reflect. The cost-effectiveness concept is less useful when it comes to choosing between systems with broadly dissimilar outputs, and this is precisely why, unless employed with intelligent regard for its necessary shortcomings, it may act as too sharp a brake on the innovating process that is concerned with radically new ideas.

Much the same point is made about the military-requirement concept:

> unless greater care is taken . . . the military requirement procedure may kill off too many new ideas *before* their value can be sufficiently established. This may happen as a result of fiscal over-anxiousness in administering the economic contraint. If the military requirement must be very clearly elaborated before the expenditures for the development of an idea or project are authorized, the economy ax may fall too readily in every case, or in most cases, of doubt. And if this happens, the procedure will favor conventional technology, for which the uses are obvious because they likewise are conventional, and will be inimical to novel ideas, whose specific military application is less immediately apparent or, more important, for which the specific application must be invented, together with the hardware.[9]

These are moderate enough criticisms hardly directed at a particular decision which the authors disliked. It is the underlying strategy or, if you will, theology which is being questioned.

We have already suggested that an attack on the problems of weapons and strategies from the standpoint of "political and military desiderata" was not a congenial stance for Mr. McNamara. The SKYBOLT affair of December 1962 can be taken as an example of this point. The SKYBOLT air-to-ground missile was designed to give an aging, subsonic strategic bomber (the B-52) added capability to penetrate sophisticated, Soviet antibomber defenses. It was not a new concept by any means; but it would constitute an improvement over the already operational HOUND DOG. In light of the failure to produce a strategic missile (BLUE STREAK) as the keystone of their deterrent force, the British saw SKYBOLT as a means to maintain the V-Bomber force in the environment of the late 1960s and 1970s. Stress has been put on Secretary McNamara's aversion to "independent" national deterrents to explain the cancellation of the air-to-ground missile and the agreement to supply it to the United Kingdom. There is little doubt about Mr. McNamara's attitude concerning multiple national deterrents, but it would be a mistake to assume that this attitude (and the decision) stemmed primarily from premises of national policy or strategy.

Two points need to be made, in conjunction with the cancellation of SKYBOLT, about the Secretary's predilections. Mr. McNamara, first of all, was always candid on the subject of collective defense undertakings and on what, in his judgment, was their most critical aspect: "the primary problem in my view is what might be called the management problem." That is to say, it is simply bad alliance management to have more than one nuclear trigger (or more than one finger on the same trigger). A strategic deterrent system must necessarily be monolithic; it must necessarily be a single-manager system. The demise of a separate deterrent force within the framework of NATO is a worthy objective, the realization of which could be hastened through the cancellation of SKYBOLT. If this view lacked political sophistication, which in short order appeared more than obvious, it was also questionable on strategic grounds. There is some indication of the latter in the Nassau Agreement of December 1962. While the agreement deprived the British of a credible strategic bomber force in the ensuing decade, it did not deprive them of a continuing, autonomous deterrent. If anything, the agreement enhanced United Kingdom "independence" in its provision to supply the British with strategic missiles (POLARIS) in place of SKYBOLT. The second point that needs to be stressed, equally as much as Mr. McNamara's notions on alliance management, is the secretary's steadfast opposition to the continuation of manned strategic systems in a deterrent force structure (whether the structure be monolithic or pluralistic). Herbert F. York in his final month as Director of Defense Research and Engineering (April 1961) reflected this aspect of the secretary's views on SKYBOLT: he told the House Appropriations Defense Subcommittee that doubts about the system were "not so much on the technical side as . . . on the question of how necessary and important the SKYBOLT is in the overall picture of providing a strategic deterrent system."[10] The question was not so much about the air-to-ground missile itself as about the manned system it reenforced. Mr. McNamara was no less hesitant about this matter than he was about the question of multiple deterrents. If anything he was more adamant about a new generation of manned bombers; independent national deterrents could be endured on the one premise that they be based on POLARIS rather than manned bombers. The wholly predictable reaction of General DeGaulle and the subsequent reemergence of the Multilateral Nuclear Force (MLF) idea confirmed the SKYBOLT affair as a kind of second Dunkirk, this time as much for Mr. McNamara's purposes as for Mr. Macmillan's. One cannot blame secretary McNamara alone for the "disarray" in NATO that followed; on the other hand, one can obtain from the SKYBOLT affair yet another view of the parameters of his decision-making thought.

The issue at hand is not one of making a determination of "stagnation" or "progress" in weapons, but one of discerning an attitude on the part of the Secretary of Defense. Among the constraints on "innovations," none would be more important than the "convictions" of Mr. McNamara. Within the framework of a logistic strategy, the secretary's bent was not toward the generation of new systems, but rather toward the implementation of existing opportunities–toward the development and refinement of weapons which were coming into the inventory in 1961. This option derived its force from the assumption that we do not live "in an age of rapid and accelerating scientific and technological knowledge." Apart from his technological "conservatism," however, Mr. McNamara's orientation to technological-logistic thought in itself (as opposed to strategic thought) remains the paramount consideration. It would color his efforts to set strategic guidelines for general nuclear war.

Assured Destruction and Damage Limitation

Building a deterrent posture around "strategic offensive forces" and, if one likes, "strategic defensive forces" did not pose the challenge for Mr. McNamara that devising a strategy or "scenario" for Central War did. The one effort was undertaken crisply as a function of management and logistics; the other posed greater uncertainties for the intellectual mode of Mr. McNamara. Since 1961, the Secretary of Defense had literally rummaged through the inventory of strategic concepts, but he did not appear to have accepted or rejected any one of them. However, by 1965 Mr. McNamara felt that he had brought the problem of general nuclear war within "a single analytical framework": this was the two-sided coin of "Assured Destruction" and "Damage Limitation."[11] There had been tentative discussions of this concept before 1965 but no full elaboration until that year. The general nuclear war forces had two strategic objectives: one, to deter a deliberate nuclear attack upon the United States and its allies by maintaining a clear and convincing capability to inflict unacceptable damage on an attacker, even were that attacker to strike first; and two, in the event a general nuclear war should nevertheless occur, to limit the damage inflicted upon our populations and industrial capacities.

It has always been easier inside the Pentagon than outside to confront the contingency of "war nevertheless occurring" in discussions of "deterrence." Still, it must be noted that in committing himself to the war objective "to limit damage," Mr. McNamara did not commit himself to a particular doctrine, strategy, tactic, or plan for achieving the objective. Conversely, none was ruled out. The situation stood in 1968 significantly unchanged from the way Secretary Gates put it in 1960: "in order to maintain a valid deterrent we have to maintain a deterrent force capable of knocking out his [the enemy's] military power and not just bombing his cities. What we would actually do depends on circumstances, but we are adjusting our power to a counterforce theory; or a mixture of counterforce theory plus attacks on industrial centers . . . what we actually do in this sort of period in a real operation is something else. I do not know for sure." [12] Mr. McNamara's quest in behalf of operational doctrine for his general nuclear war forces over the years led him to the same point. In his first major public statement (on the occasion of a University of Michigan commencement), he was clearly in search of tacit ground rules. He suggested that in response to a Soviet first strike against our military targets our response would be in kind (that is, counterforce). But the secretary could not assume that the Soviets would accomodate themselves to such rules, and, more and more, the efficacy of counterforce strikes against "hard" targets was becoming questionable. The United States would have to retain a number of options. He told the House Defense Appropriations Subcommittee early in 1964 that "regardless of whether the Soviets struck first at our cities or first at our military installations or at both simultaneously, it is probable that the launching of their bombers and missiles would extend over a sufficient period of time for us to receive the first blow, to strike back not only at Soviet cities, if that be our choice, but also at the elements of their forces that had not yet been launched." [13]

Secretary McNamara's most definitive statement on "the nature of the general nuclear war problem" was presented to the House Armed Services Committee in February 1965. It constituted the most explicit treatment by any Secretary of Defense of U.S. strategic thought on general nuclear war and the particular contingency of a failure of deterrence. At the same time, a number of issues were not fully developed, at least in the "sanitized" transcript.

Secretary McNamara spelled out the meaning of "Assured Destruction": this is the vital and paramount capability—clear and unmistakable—"to destroy an aggressor as a viable society," even after a well-planned and executed surprise attack on our strategic forces. The meaning of "inflicting unacceptable damage on the attacker," or destroying the aggressor as "a viable society," is indicated in Mr. McNamara's references to the fact that something approaching three-quarters of the industrial capacity and one-half of the population of the Soviet Union is concentrated in "the 200 largest urban areas." He relates in his statement that his calculations show that these could be destroyed by already programmed missiles which would survive a first attack. Manned bombers would not be required in the assured-destruction role except to inflict additional increments of damage—and that on a diminishing-returns basis.[14] The inescapable inference is that Mr. McNamara is speaking not only of a capability which should deter a rational opponent, but also of the mission of the strategic offensive forces in the event "war should nevertheless occur." The objective in the face of this contingency is not simply as Mr. McNamara puts it "to limit damage to our populations and industrial capacities." In point of fact, this is the second mission of strategic forces in the event of general nuclear war; the first is to operationalize "Assured Destruction" of the Soviet Union. There is eloquent testimony from the Secretary of Defense a year later to support this view: "We must, no matter what the cost, no matter what resources must be devoted to it, we must assure that the missile force is

completely reliable and can be depended upon to destroy
absolutely the Soviet Union even after we absorb a surprise
attack . . . I don't care whether it costs $1 billion or $100
billion to achieve that objective."[15] The commitment to strategic missiles to effect the assured-destruction mission without assistance from manned bombers was, of course, a commitment to MINUTEMAN and POLARIS. The "low" yield-
per-vehicle of those systems further suggests that assured
destruction is directed primarily against "soft" targets. The
nature of the Soviet first strike does not appear to be a
critical factor in determining the character of the American
response; whatever its nature, the assured-destruction objective retains priority. Conceivably a thermonuclear exchange
could stay within the Ann Arbor ground rules, where both
sides would take measured steps to disarm each other, but
only if the United States made the first strike. Apart from
that unlikely contingency, "counterforce tactics" seemed
largely obsolescent by 1965, although there might be some
place for them in the damage-limitation mission.

The objective of assured destruction had a growing operational reality behind it in 1965-66, but the second objective
of limiting damage to our populations and industries did not.
In March 1966, Secretary McNamara declared that there was
"no defense against the major threat of Soviet ICBM's," and
that he was not prepared to make a decision "to undertake
an all-out damage limiting effort against the Soviet threat."
Neither was any decision required at that time with respect
to the threat posed by Communist China. A year later, however, the secretary would find a requirement for a "thin"
ABM deployment against the Chinese threat. Mr. McNamara
advanced a number of reasons why he was not prepared to go
forward with a major "strategic program innovation" to cope
with the Sino-Soviet missile threat of the 1970s. Such a program, he argued, rested on a complex of interrelated and
interlocking factors. He granted "the high utility of a full
nationwide fallout shelter program"; it alone could be

expected to reduce fatalities by 30-40 millions at the modest cost of 5 billion dollars.[16] But against this single "constant" in the complex of factors making up a comprehensive damage-limitation program, there were a number of variables, chief among which was the antimissile missile. "A high confidence in the potential effectiveness of the system would have to be assured," Mr. McNamara insisted, before the substantial outlays that would be required could be committed. After a decade of ABM development, Mr. McNamara did not possess the necessary confidence: "there is no system or combination of systems within presently available technology which would permit the deployment now [1965] of an anti-ballistic missile defense capable of giving us any reasonable hope of keeping U.S. fatalities below some tens of millions in a major Soviet nuclear attack upon our cities."[17] The cost of deploying an ABM system and the technical problems were by no means the only factors militating against such a decision. There were even greater uncertainties about the preferred concept of deployment, the relationship of the ABM to other elements in the program, the timing of the attainment of the fallout-shelter system, and possible reactions of the enemy to deployment. In spite of a significant technological advance which gave the NIKE-X (later SENTINEL system) an area-defense capacity with long-range interceptor missiles (in addition to the originally designed terminal-interception capacity), Mr. McNamara repeated the same uncertainties again in 1966 and 1967.

The secretary was not able to determine the role of an improved manned interceptor (IMI) in a comprehensive damage-limitation program. The cancellation of the F-108 in 1959 was an early indication seemingly that antibomber defenses "no longer retain their original importance." After this decision, in which the Air Force chose to concentrate its development of "Mach III technology" on the equally ill-fated B-70, it has been a rare aircraft that has not been considered for the IMI role. Deciding upon an IMI weapon system is not as difficult seemingly as putting it into a damage-limitation posture.) General Earle G. Wheeler, Chairman of the Joint Chiefs of Staff and long an advocate of deploying an ABM system in conjunction with a shelter program, does not feel that "damage limitation" should turn on an IMI.[18] It is not clear what position Mr. McNamara held. He has stated that only if the Soviets were to increase their bomber threat "in both numbers and quality," and only if we were to decide to seek "a very large and effective damage limiting program" would "the very great cost" of deploying an IMI be justified. Whether something less than "a very large" program could proceed without an IMI remains a question. Mr. McNamara has made it clear that even then antibomber elements must be in balance with antimissile elements. There is also the possibility that he would have substituted altogether for the IMI a force of advance antibomber missiles (although the Air Force has never regarded them as equivalents).

What forces itself upon one who has followed the secretary's rather extended discussions of damage-limitation programs is his failure to expand upon the various strategic ramifications growing out of the deployment of active and passive defenses. This may result from a reluctance to do so publicly or it may reflect more fundamental objections. There is, in any case, a consistent bias for "the offense" as against "the defense" in his thought. Mr. McNamara, for example, has had a tendency to see the deployment of an ABM system by the Soviet Union as creating problems, and minor at that, for our offense, not for our defense: "their Damage-Limiting problem is our Assured Destruction problem." Comparative-cost figures (Mr. McNamara's figures) suggest one basis for the secretary's preference for offense technology over defense technology. He suggests that "at the level of spending required to limit fatalities to about 40 million in a large first strike against our cities, we would have to spend four times what the potential aggressor would have to spend on damage creating forces . . . this argument is not conclusive against our undertaking a major new Damage Limiting program . . . but it does underscore the fact that beyond a certain level of defense, the cost advantage lies increasingly with the offense, and this fact must be taken into account." By January 1967, however, the secretary would indicate that "this fact" was changing. As late as the summer of 1966, Mr. McNamara would not grant that the deployment of an ABM system by the United States would have deterrent value: "If you want to increase your deterrent, you can't add to it with Nike X." He emphasized that "the *offense* still is the key to our entire program . . . Letting the offense lag is suicide. Our continuing research and development work on Nike X assists in keeping the *offense* from lagging. In preparing experimental defense systems we learn more about penetration aids to our own offensive missiles to foil the enemy defense. That, I think, is a principal value of our Nike X research." It has been suggested that Mr. McNamara's reluctance to make "starts" on such new weapon systems as an ABM, an AMSA, or an IMI reflects an effort on his part to test out the thesis of "non-negotiated techniques" or "unilateral initiatives" in arms control. The thesis, associated especially with Mr. John T. McNaughton, late Assistant Secretary of Defense for International Security Affairs and former General Counsel, contends that such efforts on our part will result in reciprocal initiatives by the Soviet Union and others, thereby easing the arms race outside the context of a general disarmament treaty. Deputy Secretary of Defense Roswell L. Gilpatric indicated his concurrence in the thesis upon his retirement.[19]

Damage limitation inevitably brings one back to the role of the strategic offensive forces. At this point the dilemma of counterforce is painfully posed since it is clear that the *timing* of damage-limitation strikes takes on awesome importance. Secretary McNamara thought it "an unlikely contingency" that a Soviet first strike would fall only on U.S. military targets. But only if their first strike is phased, that is, with the attack on urban areas delayed, can our strategic offensive forces limit damage to population and industry to any degree through counterforce strikes. The damage-limitation burden would fall heavily on active and passive defenses which Mr. McNamara was hesitant to deploy. Retaliatory offensive forces would most likely find some "residual" military targets, but attacks on them would serve only to blunt follow-up strikes. Against the somber prospect of a minimal deployment of defensive systems coupled with counterforce strikes by the United States following an opening Soviet onslaught, Mr. McNamara has suggested in graphic terms what it would mean for U.S. damage-limitation strikes to fall *first*. Using seven different scenarios each of which assumes various levels of capability on each side, he has shown that a U.S. first strike would mean substantially fewer fatalities in these scenarios. Significantly, after a jump in the expenditure level from $25 billions to $45 billions (over ten years) in the U.S. damage-limiting posture, U.S. fatalities are down to one-third of enemy fatalities. [20] The categories "first strike" and "second strike" may well be little more than analytical devices. Except under extraordinary circumstances, a fully executed, surprise first strike by either side has little reality. On the other hand, the possibility of a half-hour "notice" is credible; in such a case counterforce tactics designed to "limit damage" are not drained of meaning.

A persistent theme in American rhetoric militates against the possibility of an American first strike. President Kennedy put stress on it in his first defense message to Congress on March 28, 1961: "Our arms will never be used to strike the first blow in any attack. It is our national tradition . . . we are not creating forces for a first strike against any other nation." [21] Whatever advantage "this may appear to hand an aggressor" would have to be offset by the building of a second-strike capability which would convince any aggressor that an attack would be "too futile and costly to undertake." Recognizing the possibility of an attack even in the face of an imposing deterrent posture, Kennedy conceded that the capability to which he referred was "that portion of our forces which survive the initial attack." Implicit in the President's remarks is the assumption that the initial attack would, indeed, fall on our strategic forces; attention is not directed to the possibility of the initial attack falling on urban areas, or the possibility that these areas would not have the benefit of significant active and passive defenses. There is some evidence that by 1965 Mr. McNamara was forced to reappraise the national tradition of no first strike in light of these considerations. A number of members of Congress were by no means persuaded of its merits and had even called upon the Department of Defense to review it.

There is symmetry in Mr. McNamara's commitment to assured destruction (a second strike by surviving elements against the social structure of the attacker) and the priority of second-generation strategic missiles. In turn, the lack of prominence for manned strategic systems in the secretary's mind stems in large part from the lack of prominence of the damage-limitation mission of strategic offensive forces. There are other cases to be made for manned systems, but the central mission of an advanced manned strategic system is the damage-limitation mission against hard military targets in the enemy's interior zone. Mr. McNamara has not been expansive on the damage-limitation role of strategic offensive forces, much less the particular role of manned systems. The secretary's strategic predilections on central war doctrine, technology, and logistics set the frame within which he would consider and rule against a follow-on manned bomber.

The Systems Inventory

During the Eisenhower years two major strategic programs were carried forward to cope with the threat of general nuclear war. The first program, which had its genesis in the Lovett term, was to build an arsenal of atomic and hydrogen weapons for strategic air warfare. The major delivery vehicle was the B-52 intercontinental jet bomber, first complementing and then gradually displacing the B-47 medium-range bomber. In the mid-1950s the Eisenhower administration further implemented this program through the introduction of intercontinental ballistic missiles. The first-generation missiles, ATLAS and TITAN, were cumbersome and had slow reaction times due largely to a liquid oxygen fuel. In their original configuration they stood "exposed" above ground; however, they had the capability of delivering major payloads (perhaps on the order of ten megatons). Toward the end of the 1950s a second generation of strategic missiles was developed. The new missiles, MINUTEMAN and POLARIS, had a solid, chemical fuel which reduced the reaction time to the order of two minutes. This vastly improved their survivability, as did the fact that they could be deployed in hardened, dispersed, and in some cases hidden sites. In what was possibly the most revolutionary development in weapons technology in the twentieth century, the strategic nuclear missile POLARIS was joined to the nuclear-powered submarine. Sixteen such missiles could be deployed under the sea in one submarine for indefinite periods of time, thereby achieving a state of high invulnerability. By 1961 six strategic delivery-vehicle types (two aircraft and four missiles) were in the inventory with production lines open. (The Mach-II medium-range B-58 bomber had been added, but at the same time the B-47 had been scheduled for phase-out.)

The second major strategic program of the Eisenhower administration was the development of a North American air defense posture. A substantial antibomber capability was achieved through elaborate warning systems, interceptors, and antiaircraft missiles. At the end of the decade a ballistic-missile early-warning system (BMEWS) was added, and a program to develop an antimissile missile (NIKE-ZEUS) was underway. The antibomber capability was enhanced by improvements in the warning net, continuing deployment of the nuclear-tipped NIKE-HERCULES, and open production lines for the F-106 interceptor. At the same time the Strategic Air Command moved back from forward bases and initiated a program to put a part of the force on alert status. Not yet at a point where definitive choices in weapon systems were considered desirable, Secretary Gates outlined the nature of our defense problem in 1960:

> the problem of maintaining our capability to deter general war has become complicated and costly because of the rapid progress in military technology . . . Programs which looked promising only a short time ago have become marginal in importance in the light of technical advances . . . we must avoid being carried away by the glittering promise of the future at the expense of present military strength—hastily discarding proved and effective weapons we actually have now for developments which may become reliable weapons in the future. Undoubtedly we have overstayed our time on some projects, but considering the program as a whole, the rate of adjustment to technological progress has been rapid and remarkable.[22]

The objective was one of shifting emphasis to the new systems and at the same time improving the reliability of older, proved systems. Mr. McNamara would find this policy redundant and expensive.

Early in 1961, Secretary McNamara undertook a "massive effort" to develop a new statement of U.S. strategic delivery requirements. The problem of national security would not be of the magnitude that President Kennedy had suggested during the 1960 campaign. As one observer put it, through a "miraculous transformation" the missile gap had disappeared.[23] From the outset Mr. McNamara chose to shift the emphasis in strategic missiles from ATLAS and TITAN to MINUTEMAN and POLARIS more rapidly than had been contemplated by the Eisenhower administration. The Secretary of Defense was enthusiastic about MINUTEMAN. It was smaller, less expensive to produce, less expensive to maintain on alert status, and it lent itself to hardening and dispersal.

The production of large numbers of MINUTEMAN would also facilitate "saturation tactics," a propensity for which Mr. McNamara quickly developed. However, in letting the ATLAS and TITAN programs run out (two TITAN squadrons were canceled also), Mr. McNamara was affecting another critical ratio, in this instance the yield-per-vehicle ratio. As early as April 1961, it was noted that exclusive reliance on MINUTEMAN and POLARIS would substantially affect the "deliverable megatonnage" of each missile as well as the total amount. Mr. McNamara agreed that the two missile generations were "apples and oranges," and that substitution on a one-for-one basis would not be appropriate. He contended, however, that the "large" ICBM's (ATLAS and TITAN) were designed for one purpose and the "small" ICBM's (MINUTEMAN and POLARIS) were designed for another. There was, apparently, an underlying strategic doctrine which called for the new mix of large and small strategic missiles. Mr. McNamara did not spell it out publicly, except to say that it involved no change in policy.[24]

In July 1965 all ATLAS and TITAN I missiles were phased out of the operational inventory without any apparent doctrinal difficulty. (A TITAN II force of fifty-four missiles remained.) In spite of this development, 1965 was a memorable year for the Air Force: for the first time there would be more missiles in the strategic inventory than aircraft. General John P. McConnell, Air Force Chief of Staff, marked the historic transition with an interesting footnote: "however, the manned bombers still carry some 80 percent of the total megatonnage currently programmed for delivery by SAC forces and will continue to carry the bulk of these weapons through 1970."[25] After an original projection in 1964 of 1,200 MINUTEMAN missiles by 1970, Mr. McNamara became convinced that a force of 1,000 missiles (in 1970) would not only be as effective but would actually have an increased total destruction capability "of at least 30 to 40 percent."[26] This calculation was based on the facts that

MINUTEMAN II became operational in October 1965 and that MINUTEMAN III would be added by 1968. Mr. McNamara was speaking now not so much in terms of saturation through numbers as he was of "qualitative improvements" such as increased accuracy, penetration aids, and multiple payloads. Whether these in turn were the result of doctrinal changes or technological opportunities was not discussed. Mr. McNamara was impressed with POLARIS as well. At the outset he would approve only a "29-boat" program but ultimately approved the Eisenhower projection of 41 boats (656 missiles). Qualitative improvements in the POLARIS missile took it through three stages; at that point Mr. McNamara ordered work to begin on a new strategic missile for the navy (POSEIDON) which, with MINUTEMAN III, would have a multiple-warhead capability (MIRV). In January 1961 there were six ATLAS missiles operational and two POLARIS submarines deployed. There was no question but that a substantial strategic nuclear offensive force of missiles with a good survival or "ride-out" capacity had been established. How this was coupled with strategic doctrinal developments will be considered below.

The production line on B-52 intercontinental jet bombers, open since 1955, was shut down by Mr. McNamara in 1962 after delivery of nearly 800 aircraft. After delivery of some eighty B-58 supersonic, medium-range strategic bombers, production of this aircraft was also closed down in 1962. In 1961 Mr. McNamara closed out production of the last operational interceptor, the F-106. The program to develop a nuclear aircraft engine (ANP) was canceled the same year for lack of a military requirement, although at the same time Mr. McNamara increased the research and development appropriation for DYNA-SOAR. This project would be defunct two years later. No new strategic bomber or interceptor went into production during Mr. McNamara's years in office. No new aircraft types were provided for the Tactical Air Command; the two mainstays in 1968, the F-105 and the F4 (developed by the Navy), came into the inventory at the beginning of the decade. In a decision which former Secretary of the Air Force, Eugene M. Zuckert, has called "probably the most typical payoff of the McNamara technique," the Secretary of Defense committed himself to the TFX.[27] At first a project to secure a tri-service tactical fighter, Mr. McNamara came to see the TFX as, additionally, a strategic bomber and an interceptor. (The fate of the TFX—or F-111—in all of its ramifications was not fully determined at the end of the secretary's term. The prospects appeared bleak.) Mr. McNamara announced in 1965 that the oldest squadrons of B-52's (the B Series) would be phased out in 1966. In January 1966 he told the Congress that 345 additional B-52's (C-F Series) and all of the B-58's would be withdrawn from the,inventory by 1971. This would leave, apart from normal attrititon and operational losses in Vietnam, some 255 B-52's (G and H Series) in the Strategic Air Command in 1971. The Secretary of Defense announced at the same time his intention of adding 210 FB-111's during the next five years. The FB-111 would be the "stretched" strategic bomber configuration of the TFX. The B-52 retirement schedule was thus pinned to the assumption that the FB-111 would in fact come into the strategic bomber inventory.

There has been a running controversy between Secretary McNamara and his critics, both in and out of Congress, on the question of "new" weapon systems or the lack of them during his tenure. The peak of the controversy was Mr. McNamara's appearance before the Resolutions Committee of the Democratic National Convention in Atlantic City on August 17, 1964. On this occasion, the Secretary of Defense reviewed the entire spectrum of defense issues in a manner inconsistent with his testimony both before and since. His address to the committee was a wholesale attack on the "judgment and competence" of his predecessors and most particularly the record of Secretary Thomas S. Gates. Mr. McNamara's sally into the political maelstrom was notable because of the fact that the Jackson Subcommittee had been painstakingly developing the point that the offices of the Secretary of State and the Secretary of Defense were, and ought to remain, nonpolitical. Arthur Krock recalled that it was the first Secretary of Defense, James V. Forrestal, who, in refusing to actively support President Truman's 1948 campaign, established the principle that Senator Jackson was so concerned to reiterate. Krock defined Mr. McNamara's action at Atlantic City as "a gross impropriety." Secretary Gates felt compelled to write a personal letter to his successor in which he pointed out that "these statements are not a true representation of the Department of Defense of which you assumed charge in 1961. Since you have often given me and the Eisenhower Administration great credit for your own policies . . . I cannot believe that you agree with these statements yourself." Obviously upset, Gates stated that "if the conditions had been as you have described them, then I could not have remained in office . . . in fact if our defense posture then had actually been in the state of disorder you have painted, I doubt that anyone could have corrected it in the time you have been in office." Responding to criticisms that had arisen especially during the 1964 presidential campaign, Mr. McNamara told the House Armed Services Committee in February 1965 (Congressman L. Mendel Rivers was in the chair for the first time), "It is idle . . . to argue about which administration is entitled to credit for this or that particular weapons system. Let it be said once and for all that the weapon systems entering our forces today are to a great extent based on the technology created during the prior administration and even the administration before that. This situation simply reflects the nature of scientific advancement. Each generation builds on the knowledge accumulated by its predecessors." Unfortunately, the secretary touched off the always simmering issue again when he told the same committee a year later, "*we* still cannot see a clear need for a new strategic bomber."[28]

Dialogue on AMSA

The issue of an advanced manned strategic aircraft (AMSA) as a follow-on in the 1970s for the B-52 is far more than a question of choosing a weapon. It is a larger and potentially more dangerous controversy than is generally appreciated. It comes as close to effecting a pure division between the civilian and the military professional as any issue in the often hectic tenure of Mr. McNamara. Many of the highly debated issues that have divided the Pentagon since 1961 have found economists, physicists, military, and budget analysts at both the office of the Secretary of Defense level and the service level on each side. In the case of an AMSA, Mr. McNamara, Mr. Gilpatric, Mr. York, Mr. Brown, and Mr. Zuckert all withheld intellectual commitment to or support for the concept. The public transcript of the McNamara years, carefully studied, admits of no other conclusion. As a result, the case for the manned bomber within the Department of Defense has had to be made by the uniformed officers of the Air Force, thus putting the argument under the inevitable pall of service parochialism. The Joint Chiefs of Staff, on occasion divided over a particular aspect of the running controversy, have maintained the validity of manned bombers into the indefinite future. In March 1966 they were united in a recommendation for the full-scale development of AMSA. Still, the burden of proof has rested exclusively with the Air Force (an object lesson in which all three services may find some profit).

In the first months of Mr. McNamara's administration, General Thomas S. White, at that time Air Force Chief of Staff, told the Congress that he was already concerned with what appeared to be a new philosophy: "it is not so much what the budget contains as some of the testimony that I have read of some of the officials who have been here . . . which present[s] the overall philosophy that manned aircraft have ceased to be of value. It is the philosophy even more than the overt decision to cut back the B-70 that bothers me, because I feel that war is an art and will always be an art."[29] White was enthusiastic about the ICBM's coming into the strategic inventory, calling them "exceptional weapons," but he believed that it was not possible for them to perform vital war functions which required "on the spot, trained human judgment." He stated the case for manned systems in terms from which the Air Force would not deviate thereafter: "there are two incontestable, overriding mandates for the continuation of manned systems. The first of these concerns the simple but awesome decision to commit the force . . . a second mandate for the manned system concerns the perpetual requirement for operational flexibility."[30]

The man "myths are made about" (not always an enviable status), General Curtis E. LeMay, who succeeded General White as Air Force Chief of Staff, spelled out the basic propositions on many occasions. He was at his colorful best, perhaps, in his final appearance before the Defense Appropriations Subcommittee of the House on February 25-26, 1964. LeMay was a man genuinely concerned.

You are endangering the defense of the country by depending on this weapon system [strategic missiles] alone because you have no flexibility. You only have two choices. You are either off the button and are at peace or you are on the button and you are at war . . . there is no loyalty to a missile. It goes where you say it should go when you launch it. You cannot change your mind and bring it back. You cannot hit imprecisely defined targets with a missile. You have to send a missile to a certain longitude and a certain latitude. Manned systems can use judgment, can find targets you know are in the area but you do not know exactly where until you go and look . . . anyone is foolish to try to sit here now and assume a method of fighting a war that may happen to us 10 years from now. I want all the flexibility in the world I can think about so that I can do something in case I am surprised, which I am sure I will be . . . I firmly believe the right answer is to have a mix of weapon systems and not depend on one . . . I say to you if you were the President of the United States and only had missiles to fire, when are you going to press that button? I say

you are going to think a long time before you do it. If you have
anything else you can use to show your will, you are going to use
it . . . the big use of these manned systems comes before the war
ever starts to show will to fight. You have flexibility . . . you have
a better chance of preventing a war with manned systems than
you do with unmanned systems. [31]

LeMay was addressing himself to the incontestable mandates, operational flexibility and the awesome decision to
commit the force. His argument was that in the deterrent
posture (before the buttons are pushed) manned systems can
effect a deterrent psychology that missiles in silos cannot.
Just as naval tactics of showing the flag through the visible
presence of warships in crisis areas have been effective, the
launching of manned bombers at critical junctures could have
the same impact. While for the rational, calculating mind the
MINUTEMAN should be sufficiently convincing, in times of
crisis the emotional factor comes to the fore and deterrence
is likely to be a function as much of emotion as of intellect in
the final analysis. By sending manned systems out to the
periphery of enemy radar, subject to recall, we might well
avoid a holocaust rather than initiate one. The argument is
not to be carried too far, nor is it to stand alone; yet it was in
any case an argument that Mr. Harold Brown, then Director
of Defense Research and Engineering, wished to respond to.
He could not agree with General LeMay about the value of
pre-attack launchings of manned systems. It was Brown's
view that "if you launch a very large bomber force, I think
you may precipitate a much bigger action than if you just
launched a single missile."[32] Brown's explanation of how the
detonation of a strategic nuclear missile in enemy territory
could be less provocative than a flight of manned bombers
approaching enemy radar was simply that a lot of accidents
could happen during the flight and that the aircraft very
likely would produce a big reaction even before reaching
their targets. The issue hinges on the question of uncertainties. Brown argues that bombers enroute to their targets

introduce more uncertainty into the very delicate war-outbreak situation than do missiles in their silos, or even one missile fired at the enemy. LeMay could not disagree more emphatically. The greatest uncertainty that could arise in a crisis situation is that the United States would not respond adequately. Bombers airborne lend more credibility to U.S. firmness than do silent silos; they allow a President of the United States more room for dramatic impact at a time which is bound to be charged with emotion. Both bombers and missiles are subject to accident; bombers alone are subject to recall. Harold Brown found the reasoning of LeMay with respect to manned aircraft (and 100-megaton bombs) essentially "psychological." His reaction was true to form: he did not mean to suggest that the reasoning was poor, but he observed that "it is hard for me to evaluate it technically."[33] It was obviously hard for the Air Force to evaluate the argument put forward by the Director of Defense Research and Engineering "psychologically."

Turning from the "awesome decision to commit the force" to the question of operational flexibility, General LeMay contended that once one is no longer in the deterrent posture but has "gone to war" it then becomes clear that manned systems alone have "the inherent flexibility and specialized characteristics" required for a number of military tasks. He could not accept the view that the problems which would confront one at the point of war outbreak had been synthesized in the single analytical framework of assured destruction and damage limitation:

> the thing that bothers me is that I do not think that any of us can sit here today and cover all the angles of things that might happen when some future war starts. *It has been my experience* that things are entirely different from the way we visualize them ... the more flexibility you have, the more capable you are of reacting to surprises when the fighting starts ... If you had all the time in the world and wanted to deliver an optimum attack, I think that would be to use your missiles to hit the targets first, followed as quickly as possible with your manned systems.[34]

One was not going to have all the time in the world, however, and he might be required to resort to "unplanned" actions. Nothing aggravated the Air Chief so much as the contention that manned systems could not penetrate the sophisticated air defense systems of the present day. Mr. McNamara told Congress in February 1964 of a study done not by the Air Force but "at OSD level." There were "two striking conclusions" which he had "no hesitancy whatsoever" in putting forward: these were (1) that a higher percentage of missiles could get through to targets than aircraft,[35] and (2) that there is greater systems dependability for missiles than for aircraft. LeMay responded in impassioned terms to the charge that aircraft could not penetrate sufficiently: "as far as I know Secretary Zuckert and Secretary McNamara have not ridden on a bomber raid as a lot of us in the Air Force have."[36] Whatever "image" LeMay might have, he was an experienced practitioner of air war and was concerned primarily with the military aspects of the problem of general nuclear war. He was afraid that much of the current thinking might be directed at "working the wrong problem":

> Our problem is not one of killing our opponents. Our problem is one to keep our opponents from killing Americans and our allies . . . If we just want to kill our opponents, that is a very simple problem. It calls for a lot less weapons than if we are trying to protect ourselves . . . what we want is to get the weapons that are going to be fired at us . . . Under most potential circumstances of war outbreak, the objective of U.S. military action would be to limit damage to the populations of the United States and its allies rather than to "annihilate tens of millions" of people in the Soviet Union. This objective is demanding in terms of forces and capabilities since it requires the effective attack of all possible military threat targets while at the same time avoiding to the fullest possible extent unnecessary collateral damage. The latter is important in order to insure that the enemy can recognize that we are not attacking his population and that we may not so long as he does not attack our cities.[37]

The essential point in a dialogue that often wandered afield was whether advanced manned strategic systems could execute missions in various threat situations of the 1970s and 1980s alone or in conjunction with missiles more effectively than could strategic missiles alone. It would be necessary to specify the missions sufficiently to bring an AMSA concept to operational reality—something which the office of the Secretary of Defense felt the Air Force had not done—and it would be necessary to be something less than rigid about plausible scenarios—something which the Air Force felt the office of the Secretary of Defense was not.

The Air Force presented a twofold argument in behalf of an advanced manned strategic system. There was a psychological contribution to deterrence that only manned systems could provide, and there was operational flexibility not available with strategic missiles. The argument, for better or worse, reflected the conclusions of wartime experience and the professional conservatism of the military. The Air Force was more than positively inclined toward strategic missiles. The advance of missile technology, however, was not eliminating manned systems; rather it was making it possible to more specifically relate various systems to roles and missions. Weapons technology had not produced a panacea for general nuclear war in the strategic missile; instead it had provided a variety of new systems, manned and unmanned, which would bring to general war a degree of flexibility and discrimination not thought possible in the aftermath of Los Alamos. Those who argued that technological proliferation imposed the stern demand of choosing on defense planners were, indeed, correct. But it was no response to this challenge simply to go it alone with ICBM's. The Air Force clearly did not accept the "logistic" premise of a technological plateau, nor was it satisfied with the "strategic" premises of Mr. McNamara's assured destruction-damage limitation dichotomy.[38]

In making the case for an advanced manned strategic system, the Air Force understood from the beginning that the office of the Director of Defense Research and

Engineering would not be a source of assistance. The first
Director, Herbert F. York, thought that on the whole aircraft
were here to stay, but that "the intercontinental strategic
bombardment aircraft is a variety which may very well become much less important and disappear," possibly by 1970.
York's AMSA concept was one of a pilot doing little "except
to check the gas tanks and punch a few buttons." As far as
the flexibility argument was concerned, getting aircraft off
the ground early and possibly later recalling them was
"simply another means for maintaining them alive"; missiles,
on the other hand, could ride out an attack.[39] No one could
be more opaque from the standpoint of the Air Staff, unless
it was York's successor, the man who ultimately would become Secretary of the Air Force. York had conceded that the
question of an advanced manned strategic system was not "a
scientific question" at bottom; Harold Brown, on the other
hand, was not reluctant to enter into the realm of strategic
doctrine and military operations to confront the Air Staff
head on. Probably the most categorical statement against
further concern with manned strategic vehicles came from
Deputy Secretary of Defense Roswell L. Gilpatric following
his retirement. He envisaged by 1970 a deterrent force con-
sisting "only of hardened and dispersed land-based and mobile sea-based missiles" with "all manned bombers retired
from active deployment."[40] Gilpatric saw the issue tied up
particularly with what the Soviets did with manned systems.
If they retired theirs, then we would be called upon to retire
ours; such an argument might well imply that since the
Soviets did not have any aircraft carriers, it was rather awkward on our part to continue to employ them. In any event,
the rigidity of the office of the Secretary of Defense on
possible employments of manned systems is reflected in
Gilpatric's views. Secretary of the Air Force Eugene Zuckert
wrote upon his retirement that "my own view, now even
stronger, since I left the Pentagon, is that a manned strategic

system is a necessary requirement for our diversified arsenal." [41] What is significant about this statement is that Zuckert leaves such a controversial issue precisely at that— making no case whatsoever for his view. It will be noted that while he has failed to argue the case for a manned strategic system, he has in a sense taken the part of his service—a responsibility which he had set for himself as Secretary of the Air Force.

From the very beginnings of Secretary McNamara's term in the Pentagon, the Air Force had put forward the concept of an advanced manned strategic aircraft (AMSA) beyond the B-70 generation. It was a concept which precluded a "stretched-out" version of the TFX. General Thomas S. White had discussed the desired characteristics of AMSA in 1961, specifically ruling out TFX as a possible implementation of the concept, [42] and his successors, General LeMay and General John McConnell, gave increasing specification to the concept. The broad outlines of AMSA are clear. It would be a "large-payload" bomber with the space necessary to carry not only a heavy internal weapon load, but all the countermeasure devices required to penetrate a sophisticated defense environment. The aircraft would carry "laydown weapons" as well as air-to-ground missile-delivered weapons. The primary mission would be the delivery of appropriate-yield nuclear weapons against military threat targets at fixed points in the enemy interior during a general war situation. AMSA would also be configured for the augmentation of theater air capabilities in limited-war situations. With a high-capability sensor load, it would have a strategic reconnaissance role over the entire globe assisted by in-flight refueling. The opposition to AMSA has taken two forms. The first was put succinctly by Mr. McNamara himself: "I am not sure there is a military requirement here." [43] The second consisted of a more elaborate opposition at the office of the Secretary of Defense level to the lack of specificity in the Air Force's position. While there has been the implication in the latter instance that if the Air Force could determine specific operational requirements (SOR) it would remove the only roadblock in the way, the Secretary of Defense had never suggested that he saw any need for a manned strategic system beyond the FB-111. Air Force reaction to demands from the office of the Secretary of Defense for specificity on the roles, missions, and technology of AMSA is best seen, perhaps, in the comments of General Bernard A. Schriever, then Chief of the Air Force Systems Command. Schriever saw the basic question as one of "how bad you want the airplane." This will determine the degree of risk you want to take. Both the Director of Defense Research and Engineering (then, Harold Brown) and General Schriever saw AMSA "safely within the science" but disagreed on the engineering involved. Brown felt "it just may not work," and it would, therefore, be risky to go into project definition. But, according to Schriever, "you are not going to develop this airplane [AMSA] on the basis of having the hardware on the shelf to engineer and put together. You are going to have to take a certain amount of technical risk."[44] General Schriever was particularly concerned with the OSD view of requirements. It was neither possible nor wise to "fix in bronze" during the pre-project definition phase such matters as "technical feasibility, technical trade-offs, selection of optimum characteristics, technical approach, cost and schedules, cost effectiveness comparisons, etc." In advance of design and production (at least of prototypes), requirements are "something that you write down as to what you would like to have"—no more. The Air Force had been engaged in prerequisite studies of AMSA with a view to leaving as much flexibility and "growth" in the aircraft as possible. Such a view ran counter to the demand from the Secretary of Defense for studies which would "make clear" the role of AMSA in advance of project definition.

A year later essentially the same issues of project definition of AMSA were before the Congress. In 1966 Harold

Brown was Secretary of the Air Force and was willing to say that the B-52G-H force "ought probably to be replaced by some other bomber."[45] This was more than Mr. McNamara was willing to say, still Mr. Brown was not willing to agree with his service Chiefs on an AMSA concept. Having taken the view that the FB-111 was a replacement only for the B-52F-G force, he did not appear to see any urgency in reaching a decision on the follow-on system which he thought the Air Force ought to have. General McConnell noted that the optimum characteristics of AMSA had been defined, and that the JCS had concurred on project definition, and he underscored the need to make "timely decisions to convert improved technology into weapon systems hardware."[46] General Schriever again emphasized that "we are in a very dynamic technological period," that in order to proceed to engineer any weapon system concept it would be imperative to maintain flexibility in specifications, allowing room for improvisation and growth.[47] The very size of the AMSA system enhanced the possibilities for continuous modification. All that was now needed was a "decision" to go ahead. The new Director of Defense Research and Engineering, John S. Foster, was "not clear" in his own mind about the two central issues—"the need" for the system and "the characteristics" of the system. Mr. Foster was especially preoccupied with the problem of penetration aids. He was not willing to say that AMSA could not penetrate, but neither was he willing to say what penetration capabilities it must have.[48] Reminiscent of Brown's bringing to Washington "a bias for nuclear propulsion,"[49] Foster states that he had brought to his job a "bias for AMSA." But as in the case of the nuclear carrier where Brown saw a lack of "systematic studies," Foster saw inadequate specifications. The viewpoint expressed by the Director of Defense Research and Engineering in 1966 (Foster) differed in no significant respect from that expressed by the Director (York) in 1961.

The AMSA question was before Mr. McNamara throughout the entire term of his stewardship of the Department of

Defense—an unprecedented seven years. During this period he continuously stood opposed to the weapon system. The question of an ABM was before the Secretary of Defense for the same length of time. Aside from the commitment to a "thin" anti-Chinese deployment (SENTINEL), he also stood opposed to this weapon system. It may be noted that part of the logic utilized by Mr. McNamara against major deployment of antiballistic missiles argued for the production and deployment of an advanced manned strategic aircraft. The secretary had insisted on the priority and the advantages of offensive weapon systems over defensive systems, yet he would not bring this consideration to bear in behalf of AMSA. If Mr. McNamara weakened on ABM, he was adamant and consistent on AMSA.

More important than decisions on specific weapon systems is the ruling conception of war in terms of which weapons choices take on meaning. It may be inferred that Secretary McNamara, after some seven years of wrestling with the problem, had not settled upon an operational notion of general nuclear war, that is, a strategic schema for the United States in the event war "should nevertheless occur." To pose the issues in a single analytical framework ("Assured Destruction"—"Damage Limitation") is not to make a decision on how to proceed; it is neither strategy nor tactics. Decisions on key weapon systems in the strategic offensive and defensive forces would be difficult indeed in the absence of a guiding concept of general nuclear war. But, again, it should not be assumed that Mr. McNamara's reluctance about AMSA, ABM, and other new systems derived solely from a disinclination for strategic thought. The secretary's cast of mind, his mode of thought, was central to be sure, but it was his conception of technology, the character of the arms race, and a managerial bent for logistical questions that emerge as the dominant considerations. "The new management" displayed a rigidity in its decision-making processes that made those decisions which posed severe tests for basic premises extend over a dangerous duration. These were invariably decisions on the most fundamental questions. The following chapter is a case study of another protracted process of decision-making. Perhaps what is most significant about the case of CVA-67 is that the decision that was finally made was a product of the new management premises; nevertheless the course of action taken was later reversed.

4

A Nuclear Carrier

 The decision to build the attack carrier CVA-67 (subsequently to be named the JOHN F. KENNEDY) with oil-fired propulsion, making it the second conventional carrier (the first was the AMERICA, CVA-66) after the nuclear-powered ENTERPRISE (CVAN-65), was a major test of the thinking and techniques of Secretary of Defense Robert S. McNamara. It provides an important case study of the convictions of the Secretary of Defense as to the validity of the new management system, not the least aspect of which was his own capacity to make a final decision. The array of opinion, from military and civilian sources alike, from inside the Pentagon and out, in opposition to this decision was unparalleled. There is little doubt that the secretary approached the issue with more confidence than experience, with more faith in his decision mechanism than in accumulated results. Perhaps the CVA-67 controversy could not and would not occur again, even during Mr. McNamara's tenure, yet it is illustrative as few incidents have been of the assuredness of the new management.

Oddly enough, the Navy did not enter into the fray with its customary assuredness. As the debate over the fiscal year 1963 attack carrier began to unfold, there was noticeable ambivalence in the Navy attitude toward nuclear propulsion for a second carrier. It was not until such external parties as the Atomic Energy Commission, the Naval Research Advisory Committee, and the Joint Committee on Atomic Energy asserted themselves that Navy ambivalence disappeared. Also notable was the fact that the Navy had allowed a doctrinal gap to develop with respect to the utilization of attack carriers (nuclear-powered carriers in particular) in likely post-World War II scenarios. This, too, would be remedied, but too late to avoid construction of an additional conventional carrier. Finally, there was early indecision about how to react to the criteria and techniques imposed by the new management, and this, in turn, was followed by clumsiness in efforts to exploit these very tools. In spite of the fact that the Navy was ill-prepared for battle, the outcome was one in which with a battle lost a war may have been won. The case for a four-reactor carrier failed not so much on its merits as because of the Secretary of Defense's lack of appreciation for such a system and the Navy's desultory efforts to remedy this lack. Significantly, no major decision taken by Mr. McNamara was followed so swiftly by steps designed to pursue the rejected course of action. The epilogue to the controversy is one in which the case for the nuclear carrier is made and a construction program started. The epilogue is one in which "effectiveness values" in cost-effectiveness analysis are seen in a new light both by the office of the Secretary of Defense, which had overplayed its hand, and by the Navy, which had underplayed its hand. The keel of CVA-67 was laid down more than two years after authorization; the intervening controversy, with the Secretary of Defense placed clearly in the eye of the storm, is the next chapter in our analysis of Mr. McNamara's decisions and the evolution of the secretarial role.

Tactical Doctrine

The attack aircraft carrier emerged from the climactic ocean war against Japan in 1945 with considerable glamor but with established credentials as well. The case for the attack carrier as a major element in the postwar American force structure, while somewhat obscured by the air power controversies of the period, was strong. In the epic confrontation of fleets in the Pacific, it was the mainstay of both sides.[1] The attack carrier and its air group (or "bird farm") were the primary striking instrument of the United States Pacific Fleet as, inexorably, they executed their primary mission of clearing the ocean of Japanese naval units. In the struggle between the fleets for control of the ocean, the attack carrier functioned as main ship of the line. Performing a classic naval role, it had a mission that was subordinated to but synonymous with that of the fleet as a whole. Marking a historic transition, the attack carrier assumed the role of the battleship, and the latter, in turn, became the major support unit of the carrier. The elimination of a large and powerful enemy combat fleet from a vast sea expanse, while not attributable to a single component of U.S. forces, did demonstrate the sweep and power of carrier air forces.

The attack carrier proved itself in ocean combat between fleets as a major attack element and as a major fleet defense element. For many this would remain the essence of the case for the attack carrier, but for others a different role appeared to have even greater significance, especially at the close of the war. The fast carrier forces of the Pacific Fleet (interchangeably organized as the Third and Fifth Fleets) demonstrated a capability to deploy rapidly to various and distant points powerful air-strike forces. The achievement of air superiority in "objective areas" and close, tactical support of forces ashore were functions of the attack carrier which loomed large at the end of the Pacific war. Contesting directly with Japanese land-based air power in the Marianas, the South China Sea, and the Ryukyus, U.S. carrier air power demonstrated that high-performance, shipboard aircraft were at no operational disadvantages; indeed, the mobility and flexibility of the attack carrier provided clear combat advantages. The basic offensive cast of American military doctrine was given new dimensions by the range and functions of the attack carrier. It was possible under cover of fast carrier forces to send ground forces to any point in the Pacific basin and to support their operations ashore. While a land-based air build-up was contemplated in such operations during the decisive phases of approach, landing, and securing footing ashore, the cover of carrier air was critical. This role, present in tactical doctrine since the advent of carriers, was superlatively confirmed in the defeat of Japan.

The decade following World War II was a bitter one for proponents of naval aviation and the attack carrier in particular. As we have seen, Secretary of the Navy James Forrestal, at the head of an imposing array of "air admirals," made the autonomy of naval aviation the *sine qua non* of Navy concurrence in any postwar reorganization of the military establishment.[2] There was complete conviction in the Navy that in the attack carrier the classic concept of ship of the line and the new modality of air power had been successfully conjoined. High-performance combat aircraft operating from fast carriers must be an essential element of the postwar force structure; the lessons of World War II would admit of no other conclusion. The Navy secured its point in the reorganization struggle, but it was a point that would have to be repeatedly defended. As late as 1963, in the clash over CVA-67, we shall see that the very existence of carriers was still an issue in the mind of the Secretary of Defense.[3] In the years immediately after World War II, the aura of strategic air power, if anything, was even more dazzling than that of carriers. The stature of strategic air power, the doctrinaire stance of some enthusiasts, the advent of nuclear weapons, and the bipolar structure of a developing Cold War forced the Navy to consider how carriers could be adapted to the strategic mission. This development on the whole had an unfortunate impact on attack carrier doctrine.

In the decade before fleet ballistic-missile (POLARIS) submarines were coming on station and when the B-52 force was not yet wholly available, U.S. commitments throughout the world required the participation of carrier air in the strategic mission. Specifically, the decision to put the United States Sixth Fleet in the Mediterranean as a stabilizing agent in the Near East and as cover for the southern flank of NATO imposed a new role. Not only were Sixth Fleet attack carriers to provide tactical support for NATO ground forces, but they were also assigned fixed-site strategic targets in their area of responsibility. The latter requirement called upon the Navy to launch heavy attack aircraft against "deep" inland targets from carriers operating in restricted sea space. The situation, while not untenable, was altogether undesirable from the standpoint of the maximization of attack carrier capabilities. The situation was only somewhat better on the northern flank of NATO, where again there was a requirement for carriers to sally from the Atlantic into the Scandinavian seas in both tactical and strategic roles. Here, the operating space was less restricted but still uncomfortable in view of the distances to be covered from carrier decks. The doctrinal difficulties posed by the requirement to participate in the strategic mission stood out clearly.[4] The operational behavior of fast carrier forces was restricted not only by the geography of the "close seas" on the flanks of NATO, but by the strategic mission of their aircraft. The development of heavy attack types was a departure in itself and was doubtful progress in the evolution of shipboard aircraft. Extensive range and a large, internal load capacity are desiderata in a strategic bomber; these simply were not achieved in the Navy's heavy attack planes. Once such aircraft are launched from a carrier on a strategic mission, flexibility, in terms of the options open to both aircraft and carrier, is less than in any other scenario. The optimal characteristics of carrier air are not utilized in the strategic role but are actually compromised. Midway into the second postwar decade, as the strategic missile force began to assume the major deterrent role, the attack carrier was permitted to stand down from the strategic mission (subject to recall).

After the digression into the strategic realm, the Navy

concentrated its efforts on two basic types of high-performance carrier aircraft. The first was a light attack type in the subsonic range in which the primary consideration was a capability to provide close troop support with variable armament loads. This capability was achieved in the A-4 (SKY-HAWK) series, followed by the A-6 (INTRUDER) and the A-7 (CORSAIR). The second type was a Mach II-plus, that is, an all-weather, air-superiority fighter which could also be configured for the fighter-bomber role. Although these requirements were imposing, they were met—beyond expectations—in the F-4 (PHANTOM). The F-4, in fact, proved to be the best multi-functional military aircraft in the world and was adopted by all U.S. services as well as by a number of allied countries.[5] Together, the two types of high-performance aircraft gave a point and direction to carrier air which it had not had since World War II. A new requirement calling for a new (third) carrier aircraft type was visible in the early 1960s. This was the requirement for an extended-range, fleet air-defense fighter to cope specifically with "stand-off bombing" attacks. The capability to missile-launch conventional bombs from aircraft hundreds of miles out from the carrier force required in turn a system that could "loiter" on the outer air-defense periphery of the fleet. A subsonic cruise capability would have to be complemented by a supersonic capability; and a much advanced air-to-air interceptor missile would be essential. The Navy, to be sure, was interested from the beginning in the TFX tri-service fighter concept, so long as it could adapt the concept to its new requirement. The difficulty lay in the process of adaptation! In any event, it was now clear in the Navy that the most effective combat utilization of the attack carrier was in tactical scenarios where local air superiority and the precision delivery of both conventional and nuclear ordnance were the critical objectives. The development of the aircraft required for these purposes was ahead of development of the carriers that would be required.

Strategic Doctrine

The strategic considerations making the attack carrier a prominent part of the American force structure are compelling. It is in strategic terms, incidentally, rather more than in tactical terms, that nuclear power represents a quantum jump for sea power. Therefore, it is something of a mystery that the Navy, always of a strategic cast of mind, did not rush to exploit this new dimension in attack carriers. We shall come back to this point, but first the barest outlines of the strategic view of the Navy are required to delineate the raison d'être of the attack carrier. If one confines himself to "global" perspective only, and presumably there is still much basis for doing so, then it is clear that the United States lies as a kind of bastion-redoubt in the World Ocean—"off-shore" from the great World Island. It is on the World Island (and littoral areas) that the principal sources of threat and support for the United States are to be found; the World Island is the critical decision area. The exploitation of the sea is the basic means of coping with the threat-support (national security) problem posed by the World Island. The seas comprise nearly three-quarters of the globe; whether they become in themselves a threat or a support depends upon the initiative and imagination of the only major oceanic power in the world.[6]

The central role of sea power in American force structure rests on the overriding need to control and to exploit the oceans in the critical relationship with the World Island. Control of the oceans in order to deny them to potential enemies as a source of threat is primary in one sense; control in order to utilize the oceans against potential threat sources is even more fundamental in the strategic thought of the Navy. If the premises of "the offense" are basic in American doctrine, then the oceans provide great opportunities for the effectuation of doctrine. If the maxim holds that one should bend every effort to determine the general terms of conflict and, to carry the point somewhat further, if one is to confront a potential enemy with a form of conflict which is not a mere reflection of his own ideas but one which lies quite outside his experience, then, again, the oceans provide opportunities to American strategists. The oceans permit the United States to project, relatively unimpeded, immense power to points of its choosing along the "rim" of the World Island. The projection of power by air is an important complement to the ocean medium but cannot be regarded as a substitute. The oceans provide not just the primary mode of transit but a congenial ground for engagement.

The supreme exploitation of oceanic opportunities is achieved in the air-sea striking power of fast carrier forces. The versatility if not the mobility of the fast carrier force exceeds that of the fleet ballistic-missile submarine, making it the premier ocean system. Participating in joint operations or acting alone, the fast carrier force lends itself to innumerable tactical scenarios. In the likely political-military environment of the 1970s, U.S. fast carrier forces are not expected to encounter serious threats at sea from surface units, although the Soviet capability has grown rapidly. The likelihood of potential enemies targeting *strategic* missiles on U.S. carriers is remote. The major threats are posed by land-based, standoff bombing attacks and submarines. The fact that no potential enemy has a major oceangoing strike force of its own is basis in some quarters for questioning American emphasis on this area and on the attack carrier in particular. The Navy response is that this argument simply focuses on one or two tactical scenarios and overlooks the strategic context which provides many vital roles for fast carrier forces. It is in the highly mobile and flexible capabilities of fast carrier forces that we confront the "continental" threats with a dimension that is unfamiliar to the enemy.

The vulnerability of the carrier to air or submarine attack which purportedly increases with the size of the vessel is, in fact, unrelated to size.[7] The level of effectiveness of fast carrier forces, their vulnerability, whatever disadvantages accrue in connection with their use turn on a far different and more significant consideration. The capacity of the attack carrier to exploit the possibilities of mobility and maneuver afforded by the ocean; the capacity to impose punishment from afloat after long transit; the staying power of the carrier in combat environments far removed from shore support—these are the issues that need to be addressed. During the Pacific war and in the postwar era, the Navy brought the art of underway replenishment and rearming to a high precision. Nonetheless, the need to "detach," to stand down from combat for resupply, was a serious offset to the effectiveness of the carrier.[8] The most sophisticated logistical techniques, it appeared, could have only limited success in coping with the problem. The revolutionary breakthrough that was needed occurred with the development of the naval nuclear reactor.

The Navy went "nuclear" in the second administration of President Dwight D. Eisenhower. With the exception of NAUTILUS,[9] nuclear submarines started coming into the fleet in 1957. Fleet ballistic-missile submarines were not laid down until 1957. In the same year the keel of LONG BEACH (CGN-9), a guided-missile cruiser, was laid down, beginning the nuclear-propulsion program for surface units. Construction began on the first nuclear-powered attack carrier, ENTERPRISE (CVAN-65), in 1958, and the first nuclear-powered guided-missile frigate, BAINBRIDGE (DLGN-25), followed in 1959. In the final budget preparation of the Eisenhower administration (fiscal year 1962), a seven-frigate program was developed. However, the new Secretary of Defense, Robert S. McNamara, did not include a frigate in his first budget requests. One was added by House action in May 1961 (TRUXTON, DLGN-35).[10] This brought the nuclear surface ship construction program to an end. A five-year hiatus, lasting until authorization of CVAN-68 (fiscal year 1967), would be in large part the result of lagging doctrine for nuclear surface units. Only in the area of shipboard aircraft development was the new era for attack carriers beginning to come into focus.

Once the attack carrier was relieved of the strategic mission, the task before the Navy was to give precision and substance to carrier doctrine. The general euphoria over the wartime success of carriers and the postwar preoccupation with 'strategic air power had allowed doctrinal gaps to open. The Navy had not given sufficient attention to the political-military environment of the 1960s and 1970s, specifically to the tactical scenarios of the period in which the attack carrier would be the principal strike system. Secondly, there was little analysis of the implications of nuclear propulsion for carriers. Strangely enough, there was still a hesitancy at the beginning of the 1960s to focus on limited-war roles and to emphasize the operational advantages of nuclear power. It may be argued that the Navy still felt that the carrier needed to be defended on all fronts, not just in "limited"-war terms, and that prior to operating experience with a nuclear carrier (for example, the ENTERPRISE in the Cuban missile crisis of October 1962) the commitment to nuclear power must be hedged. Perhaps the best summary of the Navy's position before the Cuban missile crisis is contained in the remarks of Secretary of Defense Thomas S. Gates before the House Defense Subcommittee on January 14, 1960: "We do not believe that the carriers are obsolete. We believe that, in many respects, they are the country's best limited war capability . . . I think we would know more about the nuclear carrier when it is operational than we do now. The advantages may be so great that, if we ever build another carrier, we might want to build a nuclear one."[11] Gates would wait until operational experience was at hand to decide finally on additional nuclear carriers, but there would not at any time be any doubt about the utility of the attack carrier. Nonetheless, the task of doctrinal development was before the Navy, and hesitancy would prove costly.

In turning to the confrontation between Mr. McNamara

and the Navy in the case of CVA-67, we can shed some light on what has been referred to as a growing crisis of confidence within the Department of Defense.[12] As we shall see, it is not precisely a confrontation between civilians on the one hand and military professionals on the other; nor is it a conflict between "scientists" and "nonscientists." In the simplest terms, it is a confrontation between those who would expand the application of cost effectiveness because of its putative scientific character—and thus its presumed universal applicability—and those who would insist on a methodological pluralism in coping with the issues of national security. In the present instance, the Secretary of the Navy, his assistant secretaries, his scientific advisor, the Chairman of the Atomic Energy Commission, and the Chief of Naval Operations are united in taking exception to positions developed in the office of the Secretary of Defense. The reply may be made that this union simply reflects the parochial viewpoint of a single service arrayed against the overview of a higher level of authority. However, the point remains that the Navy case cut across professional military, scientific, and managerial opinion. That it was not enough to dissuade the Secretary of Defense is basis for the most careful assessment of the new management system.

The Case of CVA-67

The first, complete "McNamara budget" (fiscal year 1963) went to Congress early in 1962 and included a recommendation for construction of an attack carrier (CVA-67). The recommendation for a conventionally powered carrier had the support of the Secretary of the Navy and the Chief of Naval Operations. Two considerations compelled the support of Secretary Korth and Admiral Anderson, neither of whom would amass a record of unblemished concurrence with the Secretary of Defense. The first was money, and the second was a continuing ambivalence in the Navy about nuclear power. After the first year under Secretary McNamara and three revisions of the Eisenhower budget (fiscal year 1962), in which, as the then Chief of Naval Operations put it, "there was something for everyone," the new management regime took hold.[13] The fiscal year 1963 defense budget stands as the model of McNamara "systems" (or as a nice example of "early Hitch").

The Navy was off balance in its response to the planning-programming-budgeting system of the new management and appeared to convince itself that the cost of a nuclear carrier "at this time" would be exorbitant. Secretary Korth saw the cost differential as "one-third to one-half more." Admiral Anderson told the House Armed Services Committee of a simple "lack of money."[14] The problem of steadily increasing costs for each additional combat ship added to the fleet, and of the effect this would have on the overall number of units in the operating forces, had been before the Navy throughout the postwar era. It is not at all surprising, consequently, that it had difficulty in developing a united front on a question of such import. The innate conservatism that is integral to competent military professionalism urges the view that "you have a deck out there"—it is not unimportant what is below (what kind of a propulsion system you have), or what you have topside (the specific military characteristics of the ship), but these considerations are secondary. Those who adhere to this viewpoint observe that no matter how superlative a single ship may be, it can only be in one place at one time. On the other hand, there is the view that what is crucial, especially for a country with the resources of the United States, is maintaining "a decisive edge in performance" for all systems. Admiral Arleigh Burke is associated with the first viewpoint,[15] Vice-Admiral Hyman G. Rickover with the second.[16] Paul H. Nitze, successor to Secretary Korth, would look back on this episode with anguish, especially at the inability to apply "effectiveness values" correctly. In a memorandum to the Secretary of Defense, dated November

13, 1964, Secretary Nitze wrote: "The failure of operations analyses so far has been to place the correct effectiveness values on (1) being free operationally of the requirement for logistic fuel support—particularly in conflict, (2) the ability to operate warships reliably over long periods of time at high sustained speeds and (3) the strategic and tactical gain of eliminating a major at-sea replenishment requirement, e.g., continuously used ship fuel oil."[17]

The Navy went on record as opposed to a second nuclear-powered carrier until the first one (ENTERPRISE, CVAN-65) had been thoroughly evaluated. This stance was taken in the face of testimony that nuclear propulsion was "the greatest single achievement in the history of the Navy" (Anderson), and that "we fully recognize the operational benefits to be derived from a nuclear carrier" (Korth).[18] The stance was awkward, but it would be the last such performance before Congress on the part of the Navy. Signaling what lay ahead, Congress added a nuclear-powered frigate to the fiscal year 1963 budget without benefit of a request from the Secretary of Defense. In January 1964, Mr. McNamara canceled the frigate, stating that the TYPHON antiair warfare missile system intended for the frigate was behind schedule.[19] The nuclear-powered frigate TRUXTON (DLGN-25), a congressional creation of the previous year, would be the last nuclear surface unit for five years.

The fall of 1962 was a turning point. The Cuban missile crisis presumably gave a new cast to U.S.-Soviet relations; there is no question that it resolved the indecision in the United States Navy about nuclear propulsion for attack carriers. The performance it was looking for and fully expected from ENTERPRISE was provided in a "live" scenario. Vice Admiral John T. Hayward, commanding Task Force 135 which included the ENTERPRISE and the Forrestal class carrier INDEPENDENCE, played a crucial role during the crisis. Admiral Hayward submitted his findings in a letter to Secretary Korth shortly afterwards.[20] This was one of three letters at the turn of the year which had the effect of putting the Navy resolutely on course. The others were from D. E. R. Piore, Chairman of the Naval Research Advisory Committee (NRAC), to Mr. Korth and from Glenn Seaborg, Chairman of the Atomic Energy Commission (AEC), to Secretary McNamara. The NRAC, speaking through its chairman, urged that "all future major combatant ships have nuclear power plants." Piore was particularly harsh about "detailed analysis" which confuses issues and holds back "bold technical decisions." On this issue there had been sufficient analysis.[21] Seaborg, who had visited ENTERPRISE at sea after the missile crisis, specifically raised the possibility of reconsidering the decision to build CVA-67 with oil-fired propulsion. Referring to AEC's design and development program, Seaborg told McNamara of "a significant advance in technology" that made possible a four-reactor carrier at one-third less the cost of the eight-reactor ENTERPRISE. Seaborg concluded that "our own experience in this field indicates that the program has reached a stage of maturity and of promise that would justify consideration by the Department [of Defense] *of a significant increase in the application of nuclear power to the surface fleet.*[22] It was Admiral Hayward's report of the operational behavior of ENTERPRISE off Cuba that was no doubt decisive. Along with NRAC Chairman Piore, the Admiral would also have some comments on "analysis." Hayward stressed that

My experience in ENTERPRISE to date has convinced me more than ever that the military advantages of nuclear propulsion in surface combatant ships more than outweigh their extra cost ... ENTERPRISE outperforms every carrier in the fleet ... In Washington these often cited advantages of nuclear propulsion seem to get lost in a shuffle of paper—off Cuba they were real ... I have learned, often through bitter experience, that real improvements in our hardware are only made through building and evaluating in service ... my experience tells me that nuclear propulsion offers the Navy tremendous military advantages that will be sorely needed in the years ahead ... I am deeply disturbed that we are not exploiting to the fullest the technological advantage we hold in nuclear propulsion ...I do not believe you can weigh victory or defeat on a scale of dollars and cents—yet the margin between victory and defeat in future naval engagements may well depend on the availability of nuclear-powered ships.[23]

Buttressed with "combat reports" from ENTERPRISE and imposing scientific opinion from "outside," Secretary of the Navy Korth addressed the Secretary of Defense in terms far different from those of a few months earlier. After a "review of all pertinent considerations," Korth asked Secretary McNamara, "as a matter of urgency," to reconsider the case of CVA-67.[24] The four-reactor carrier referred to by Seaborg was specifically put forward as the alternative consideration. Secretary McNamara was a whole month in replying to this matter of urgency put before him by the Secretary of the Navy, as he was in replying to Chairman Seaborg's suggestion. Responding first to the AEC chairman, Mr. McNamara revealed that "we are reconsidering our decision to build CVA-67 as a conventionally powered ship ... It is being pursued *as a matter of urgency.*"[25] Mr. McNamara's reply to Secretary Korth three weeks later indicated that a good deal more thought had been given to the matter at the office of the Secretary of Defense level:

I do not feel that the subject of nuclear propulsion for surface warships has yet been explored sufficiently to permit a rational decision [on nuclear propulsion for CVA-67]... I am sure you realize that they [Navy arguments for nuclear propulsion in CVA-67] *depend upon the assumption that the future Navy will, indeed, make full use of nuclear power.* It is precisely this question which lies at the heart of the matter; far more so than the question of whether CVA-67 itself should or should not be nuclear powered. Accordingly, *I should like you to undertake a comprehensive, quantitative study of this matter* ... As a general guide, I am interested in achieving the most efficient possible naval forces, *defining efficiency as achieving the most beneficial military results for a given expenditure* ... I am reserving decision on the question of nuclear propulsion for CVA-67. [26]

The Secretary of Defense had shifted ground in the interim between his reply to Seaborg and his reply to Korth. In the former, Mr. McNamara is very brief and makes reference only to the question of CVA-67. In the latter, the question is one of the entire nuclear future of the Navy, a question requiring "a comprehensive, quantitative study." Some marked this as the end of the reconsideration of CVA-67 rather than the beginning.

Secretary McNamara agreed in February 1963 to reserve decision on the question of nuclear propulsion for CVA-67 because a larger question was still unanswered in his mind. He was not prepared at this date to assume that the future Navy would make "full use of nuclear power." It was to this matter rather than the specifics of a four-reactor carrier that he directed the Navy's attention. The secretary, adhering to the role he had set for himself, defined the terms within which the Navy inquiry must proceed: "As a general guide, I am interested in achieving the most efficient possible naval forces, *defining efficiency as achieving the most beneficial military results for a given expenditure.*" It is more than probable that the Navy did not understand this directive and even more probable that the Secretary of the Navy did not understand the Secretary of Defense. Secretary Korth submitted the "First Navy Study" to Mr. McNamara in April. This time, he took only two weeks to respond. The study was rejected. Mr. Korth reported his belief that "we have sufficiently resolved those major questions you have raised." He concluded that "nuclear propulsion does permit a significant increase in the beneficial military results for a given expenditure," and that not only CVA-67 but all new major warships should be nuclear powered.[27] The Secretary of the Navy was jubilant rather than optimistic. Whatever thoughts the Secretary of Defense may have had about the conclusions of the "First Navy Study," he kept them to himself. The study clearly did not conform to the methodology he had spelled out in February and consequently was unacceptable. Mr. McNamara's response to the study took the form of a more elaborate explication of the required procedures. Pointing to the failure on the part of the Navy to identify the magnitude of "the increase in effectiveness associated with nuclear propulsion," he went on to say that "while I realize that there are many issued involved here which are not subject to rigorous quantitative analysis, a systematic exposition of those issues which are quantifiable is necessary if I am to appreciate fully your position."[28] The Secretary of Defense having provided a specific guide for a second study provided still further assistance: the Office of Systems Analysis in the Office of the Comptroller would work with the Navy in the development of the next report.

The "Second Navy Study," done under the direction of Rear Admiral T. F. Connolly, Strike Warfare Division, Office of the Chief of Naval Operations, was forwarded to the Secretary of Defense in September 1963.[29] The second study was comprehensive and detailed. It focused on the lifetime cost differential of a nuclear-powered and a conventionally powered task force. While there was a differential on the order of 3 percent in favor of the conventionally powered task force, the advantages afforded by a nuclear-powered force made it superior in the judgment of the Navy. This was especially true, Admiral Connolly maintained, if you were talking in terms of a force level of fifteen carriers. Secretary McNamara rejected the "Second Navy Study." Unaccompanied by supporting data of his own, Mr. McNamara asserted "I am absolutely certain of one thing, that the six conventional task forces are superior to five nuclear task forces."[30]

The die was cast. The Navy had taken a "hard" position on the broad question of application of nuclear power to future major surface units and on the immediate question of CVA-67. The number of combat units in the operating forces must be determined on the basis of the military requirements of the United States as dictated by shifting international contingencies—the minimum force, under existing circumstances, not to fall below 800 ships. The quality of the ships must be such as to provide "an edge in performance" that is decisive in the most critical, and often unforeseen, circumstances. The Navy must make the transition to nuclear propulsion both in submarine and surface vessels and must build into each new ship those military characteristics which reflect the maximum state of the art. These are steps to be taken forthwith and must not wait until solely economic criteria are favorable. What is, in all events, unacceptable is the construction of a ship that is obsolete, as measured against the existing state of the art, before it is launched. If it is the case that certain nations cannot afford to take such a position, this does not hold for the United States. The Navy put forward supporting evidence which may have been both belated and unsophisticated but which was regarded, nonetheless, as sufficient.

Mr. McNamara took the position that the Navy "analysis" was insufficient. In rejecting the second study, he told Secretary Korth that his concern from the outset was with "a general policy issue" and that this issue had not been resolved. As for the fiscal year 1963 carrier (CVA-67), the Secretary of Defense took a new tack. He suggested that "the state of the legislative calendar" and "the previously expressed attitudes . . . of certain key congressional leaders" made the prospects for a change to nuclear propulsion doubtful. However this may be regarded as a reading of congressional temperament, the secretary's objective seemed clear enough. Secretary Korth must understand that Congress is committed to conventional power for CVA-67, and he is "to proceed with the construction as soon as possible."[31]

Secretary McNamara rejected Navy analysis of the issue of CVA-67 and ordered construction on a conventionally powered basis on October 9, 1963, in a memorandum to Secretary of the Navy Fred Korth.[32] On the same day Senator John O. Pastore, Chairman of the Joint Committee on Atomic Energy, wrote to the Secretary of Defense specifically asking him whether he had decided against nuclear propulsion for CVA-67.[33] Senator Pastore noted that he had been advised many months earlier that he would be kept informed of the reassessment of this question. He asked for copies of the studies that had been made and informed the secretary that the Joint Committee would hold hearings soon on the matter of nuclear propulsion for naval surface vessels. Two days later, on October 11, 1963, Deputy Secretary of Defense Gilpatric replied to Senator Pastore for Mr. McNamara. Mr. Gilpatric wrote that "final decision with respect to the type of propulsion to be installed in the aircraft carrier authorized by Congress in fiscal year 1963 *has not yet been made*."[34] Secretary of the Navy Korth understood the October 9, 1963, memorandum from the Secretary of Defense clearly enough. He responded the next day, October 10: "I was surprised to receive your memorandum of October 9 in which you asked me to take the proper steps to proceed with construction of the fiscal year 1963 carrier with conventional power rather than nuclear power . . . I earnestly request that you reconsider the decision on the method of propulsion for the fiscal year 1963 carrier . . . based on the shipbuilding program you have proposed there will not be another opportunity to build a nuclear surface ship for several years."[35] Secretary McNamara's reply to Mr. Korth's request of October 10 is dated October 25.[36] It is the "final" statement of the Secretary of Defense prior to the hearings convened by the Joint Committee on Atomic Energy. This statement is important in that it contains a number of assertions that will be directly contradicted by the Joint Committee in its report. Mr. McNamara states again on October 25 that Mr. Korth is to take steps immediately to initiate construction of a conventionally powered CVA-67. (On October 22, Senator Pastore had written to Mr. Harold Brown, Director of Defense Research and Engineering, of his pleasure on learning from Deputy Secretary Gilpatric that reports that CVA-67 was to have conventional power were incorrect.)[37] And once more the Secretary of Defense stated the issue in his terms: "the real choice we face is not between a given number of conventional ships for one sum of money and the same number of nuclear ships for a larger sum. The choice is between a given number of conventional ships and a smaller number of nuclear ships at the same total cost."[38] Mr. McNamara again insisted that the Navy position that five nuclear task forces are as good as six conventional task forces was "not generally valid." He went into detail about comparative transit times, deployment of carriers with amphibious forces, and the "logistics tail" involved. None of the points developed by the Secretary of Defense in his "analysis" would prevail in the hearings: his decision would prevail.

It was evident from the outset of the Joint Committee on Atomic Energy hearings on nuclear propulsion for naval surface vessels that matters of far-reaching import were to be aired. Senator Jackson voiced his impression that "the nuclear carrier . . . is all mixed up with the question of how many carriers or whether you should have any carriers in the future."[39] Jackson thought this was a mistake, as did most of the other members of the committee, but this did not preclude considerable discussion directed to the overall justification of surface ships in the future. Senator Jackson asked Admiral David L. McDonald, Chief of Naval Operations, whether the Navy-prescribed force level of fifteen attack aircraft carriers was being altered by the office of the Secretary of Defense. Admiral McDonald confirmed that the office of the Secretary of Defense had some questions about the figure of fifteen and described what he called the "normal procedure" for establishing force levels: "Here is exactly what happened, Senator. The Defense Department [office of the Secretary of Defense] proposed or let us look at a force level. We told them what we thought about it. They looked at our comments and then they sent this force level to the Joint Chiefs of Staff. The Joint Chiefs of Staff put their comments on it and it has gone back to the Secretary of Defense."[40] This was October 30, 1963, and Admiral McDonald was confident about getting office of the Secretary of Defense approval for fifteen attack carriers. On February 20, 1964, the Secretary of Defense told the Defense Appropriations Subcommittee of the House that "by the early 1970s we plan to make some reduction in the number of attack carriers."[41] Under questioning a few days later before the same subcommittee by Congressman William E. Minshall (R-O.) and Congressman Gerald R. Ford (R-Mich.), Mr. McNamara stated that the reason a reduction would be made in the carrier force was "because an analysis of the requirement indicated to the Chiefs that   [*deleted*] was a proper number." (He added after further questioning that "the Chiefs split on this issue rather widely.")[42] It would appear that Mr. McNamara and Admiral McDonald were not in agreement as to what constituted "normal procedure" for the establishment of force levels, Mr. McNamara leaving the impression of a Joint Chiefs of Staff decision, Admiral McDonald leaving the impression of an office of the Secretary of Defense decision.

The debate on nuclear propulsion for a second carrier, therefore, took place against the backdrop of a force-level decision on carriers which made it difficult to focus on the merits of the immediate question. Mr. McNamara told the Joint Committee that whether any new carrier at all was needed "is really the basic question," not what kind of propulsion system it should have.[43] Four months later, the celebrated Admiral Rickover, in a discussion with Congressman Melvin R. Laird (R-Wisc.) and Congressman Gerald R. Ford before the Defense Subcommittee of the House, conjectured that CVA-67 "might be the last carrier we build." In response to Mr. Ford's question as to why we would build an obsolete ship, Admiral Rickover offered the following significant, but not widely noted, explanation: "It may be that the Secretary of Defense thinks that the surface Navy should be drastically reduced and if we build this ship as a nuclear carrier, we enhance the chances for a new surface Navy." [44] Some indication of the secretary's thinking in this regard—some indication of what lay behind the decision to cut back on the attack carrier force—can be gained from two themes in his testimony. First, in his approach to determining the military requirements for an attack carrier—the needs the United States might have for such a system—Mr. McNamara spoke only of contingencies involving the Soviet Union. (Whatever his innermost thoughts might have been, there is no statement by the secretary, in which he is considering the attack carrier as part of the force structure of the United States, where he does not confine himself exclusively to threats posed by the Soviet Union.) The scenarios envisaged by the Navy, on the other hand, including specifically those drawn by Secretary of the Navy Paul Nitze, are much broader in scope and, in fact, concentrate on contingencies arising in the Pacific and Far East as the result of Communist Chinese action. [45]

In his insistence on putting conventional power into CVA-67, Mr. McNamara argued that "the substitution of a nuclear-powered carrier for the conventional would not strengthen us vis-a-vis *to the Soviets* [sic], I say this because with the total force we have available we are *in our opinion, completely protected against Soviet military and political pressure and we don't need additional force.*" [46] And later he remarked, "The aircraft carrier is not going to help us counter the *Soviet* submarine fleet. It is the *Soviet* submarine fleet that we have to be concerned with, not the *Soviet* surface fleet or not the *Soviet* forces that an aircraft carrier would attack." [47] It was not only the preoccupation of the secretary with Soviet threats or the lack of them that concerned the Navy but, more importantly, his estimation of the military worth of the attack carrier. The second point in Mr. McNamara's testimony was his contention that the vulnerability of carriers had increased. This was "because of the possible use against them of long-range *Soviet* aircraft with stand-off missiles . . . There are two circumstances I think you can anticipate developing between now and 1970. One is more *Soviet* nuclear-powered submarines. The other is greater *Soviet* capabilities for long-range reconnaissance and long-range attack. These later capabilities endanger an aircraft carrier substantially." [48] Mr. McNamara added that it was "not at all clear" to him either that a nuclear carrier would be any less vulnerable than a conventional carrier. [49]

As the discussion narrowed to the question of whether CVA-67, first authorized in the fiscal year 1963 budget, should have nuclear power as did the ENTERPRISE (CVAN-65) or oil-fired power as did the AMERICA (CVA-66), one basic point had been established. Mr. McNamara, on the basis of cost-effectiveness analyses in the office of the Secretary of Defense, was diminishing the role of the weapon system which was still central to American sea power in the judgment of the Navy. The Secretary was especially pointed on the issue of a second nuclear carrier. While granting there was "a definite additional effectiveness," his final position was that "we don't need the additional performance." [50] The United States would take the unprecedented step of undertaking a naval construction program in which ships would be built, deliberately and consciously, short of the proven state of the art. It would be fully understood from the beginning that CVA-67 would be inferior to CVAN-65. What is most remarkable, and perhaps of most concern, about this development is that it took place in spite of practically unanimous professional opinion to the contrary. When asked by Senator Pastore who shared his judgment that we do not need the additional performance of a nuclear carrier (Mr. McNamara had stated that his opinion was "shared by others"), the secretary mentioned only the name of one Air Force General. [51]

During the often heated hearings, Congress and the public learned just how insistent Mr. McNamara was on applying his analytic techniques to the broadest issues of sea power. And if there had not been doubts about the secretary's understanding of sea power among ranking officers of the Navy before fall 1963, they were raised during these hearings. Mr. McNamara told the Joint Committee that "the problem we face in the Navy . . . is the problem of pricing the Navy out of the market. There are other ways of doing these jobs. Not all of them. The Navy has absolutely unique capabilities in certain areas. In other areas it is in competition with other forms of power. The best illustration is the POLARIS. The POLARIS is not unique. The POLARIS is a substitute for other forms of strategic power."[52] Mr. McNamara saw the Navy making a contribution to the "Strategic Nuclear System," or "Central War Offensive Program," but this was a contribution for which Air Force systems could, presumably, be substituted. A fair influence, it seemed, was that in Mr. McNamara's mind a missile is a missile whether it is deployed at a fixed-point site in Montana or is mobile beneath the Norwegian Sea. The role of sea power in the latter instance would not appear germane to the secretary.

To illustrate his point about the Navy "pricing itself out of the market," Mr. McNamara cited the example of increased costs for destroyers and destroyer leaders fitted out with nuclear propulsion and guided-missile systems. What these increased costs are, precisely, was a matter of great controversy during the hearings. It will be noted that the Joint Committee on Atomic Energy in its final report pointed to a dubious use of figures by the office of the Secretary of Defense and, on the whole, concurred in cost estimates submitted by the Navy Department.[53] Likewise, it should be noted that the two members of the Joint Committee most disturbed by the secretary's use of cost figures were members otherwise well disposed toward the administration, namely, the Chairman, Senator John O. Pastore of Rhode Island, and Senator Henry M. Jackson of Washington, Chairman of the Military Applications Subcommittee. Without using any of the contested figures, we are still able to grasp the secretary's approach to the "problem of the Navy": "We have gone from x to y-million [in destroyer costs]," he told the committee. "What kind of a Navy can you have? Do you say we should have the same number of ships when they cost y-million? . . . The question is, is that the way to defend this country, with a y-million [destroyer], or is there some other way to defend this country better for y-million? . . . We just cannot build an 800-ship Navy if it is going to include y-million dollar [destroyers] . . . It just can't be done and it should not be done . . . It is just wrong to do that. There are better ways of defending the country than that."[54] Mr. McNamara was convinced that, "at today's prices," we are forced to reexamine the whole notion of sea power—indeed, more than that—"at today's prices" there *are* better ways of defending the country than with an 800- to 900-ship Navy.[55] Except for an obvious predilection for strategic missiles, Mr. McNamara did not delineate better ways of fulfilling the missions heretofore associated with sea power.

Harold Brown, Director of Defense Research and Engineering, told the Joint Committee that he, too, thought nuclear power in an attack carrier was better than oil-fired power, but that this was merely a "prejudice" of his unsupported by proof.[56] He had seen a lot of studies and analyses, had heard the testimony of many "distinguished" naval persons, but had found no proof. Brown observed that "nuclear propulsion may provide a means of achieving a major increase in the combat capabilities of surface warships, as it has done in the case of submarines, but it is not certain at this time that such will be the case."[57] (The time of which Mr. Brown is speaking here, when it is not yet certain that nuclear power would provide a major increase in combat capability for carriers, is *after* the operating experience of the ENTERPRISE in the Cuban missile crisis of 1962.) If the studies Mr. Brown had seen and the testimony he had heard, particularly that of Vice-Admiral John T. Hayward who had commanded the ENTERPRISE Task Group during the missile crisis, did not constitute proof, what then would be "proof"?, Chairman Pastore asked. [58] In reply, Brown shifted from the issue of a one-for-one comparison of nuclear and conventional carriers to argue that the "key question" was whether the increased effectiveness of nuclear-powered carriers (which, as a matter of prejudice, he would grant) would outweigh the disadvantages of a reduced number of carriers. It will be recalled that it was in precisely these terms that Mr. McNamara insisted on viewing the question. This rankled the committee. Why the assumption of reduced numbers when contemplating nuclear carriers? The reply: in our analyses we assume a fixed amount of resources available and nuclear carriers will mean higher unit costs and therefore fewer units. Chairman Pastore was more than rankled now. He told Mr. Brown that it was the prerogative of Congress to determine what the available resources were and that he was not receptive to policy declarations from the office of the Secretary of Defense as to the resource frame within which they were to work. [59] Mr. Brown, civilian manager, was being told in a fairly straightforward manner that his competence lay within the realm of scientific advice. Mr. Brown, once again the scientist, suggested that "proof" would require "further study" and that sophisticated analyses of a range of problems were needed before any decision could be made.

Senator Jackson took his turn again to express exasperation. Just why were all these additional studies required before one additional vessel could be authorized? Would not an ongoing program of design and construction followed by operational experience add to the realism of the analyses— quite apart from adding to the military capabilities of the nation? [60] Mr. Brown saw no necessity to design and build in order to enhance the studies or add to the military capabilities of the nation. He then offered an example of the kind of analysis he had in mind which should precede a decision on additional carriers. It was an unfortunate few minutes for the Director of Defense Research and Engineering. Mr. Brown, now naval strategist, spoke of an amphibious operations scenario in which the greater sustained speed of the nuclear carrier over the conventional would be of no advantage since both were considerably faster than amphibious assault ships. [61] Asked for his response to this, Admiral Hayward told the committee that Harold Brown, as naval strategist, did not know what he was talking about. Fast carrier forces are not governed in their support of amphibious operations by the speed of the amphibious vessels. It is not necessary to detail the demolition of Mr. Brown's scenario, except to say that it was complete. [62] Mr. Brown advanced another example. He spoke of a scenario in which a nuclear carrier and a conventional carrier have been steaming toward an objective area for five days. At this point the conventional carrier is only four hours astern of the nuclear carrier—it is after some additional days that a decisive gap develops between them, he contended. What was Admiral Hayward's response to this? [63] The professional naval officer first observed that he had made high-speed runs across the Atlantic with both a conventional and a nuclear carrier and that Mr. Brown's scenario and reality were two different things. Mr. Brown had assumed total availability and perfect positioning of underway replenishment ships in keeping his conventional carrier only four hours astern of the nuclear after five days; this is not a warranted assumption in peace or war. In his transit of the Atlantic with a conventional carrier, Admiral Hayward reported, the sea was so rough he could not refuel underway nor could he bring his escorts alongside for their refueling from the carrier. In fact, the carrier was burning aviation fuel before it reached its destination. Cruising range, not speed, was the decisive factor. [64]

In its report following the hearings, the Joint Committee on Atomic Energy had specific conclusions and recommendations: "On the basis of its investigation, the committee concludes that the decision announced by the Secretary of Defense on October 25, 1963 [see Appendix], against the utilization of nuclear propulsion in the next aircraft carrier, CVA-67, *was incorrect* . . . such a decision means that the Navy may be committed to a future of planned obsolescence with grave implications for national security."[65] The Joint Committee referred with obvious disdain to the "cost effectiveness comparisons made within the Department of Defense"; the logistics assumptions were a defect in the analysis that was "immediately apparent." The proposition that the logistic support forces would operate "unhampered and without losses" was untenable in the opinion of the committee. Moreover, the Department of Defense had overestimated the cost of nuclear propulsion for surface warships. In any event, "even if a somewhat higher cost is incurred to pay for the increase in military capability," this cost is nothing against national security needs.[66] The Joint Committee again made reference to Mr. McNamara's proposition that conventional propulsion would mean more ships: "The committee was told that the choice we face is between a given number of conventional ships and a smaller number of nuclear ships for the same total cost. In other words, to improve a weapons system we must reduce the number of weapons to pay for it. The committee does not share this view . . . this could create an intolerable peril to our national security."[67] The Joint Committee recommended: (1) that the secretary's decision be set aside and nuclear propulsion be put in CVA-67; (2) that the U.S. utilize nuclear propulsion in all future "major surface warships"; and (3) that a "vigorous" research and development program to bring about this end be pursued.[68]

Four months after the Joint Committee's report, the House Appropriations Committee brought the defense appropriations bill for fiscal year 1965 to the floor; it did not include a recommendation for funds to convert CVA-67 to nuclear propulsion. Unmoved by the force of the JCAE report, the Secretary of Defense did not ask for additional funds "for the previously funded ship." In the absence of such a request—and in the absence of authorization by action of the Armed Services Committee—the Appropriations Committee took no action. [69] More than a second nuclear carrier had been lost. Mr. McNamara reported to the Defense Subcommittee of the House that because of the delay in the start on CVA-67 the attack carrier previously programmed for fiscal year 1965 was canceled. [70] In no mood for more delay, the Navy and the Congress concurred in the standing order to proceed with construction on a conventionally powered basis.

Two weeks after the Appropriations Committee report (on April 30, 1964), the contract was let to Newport News Shipbuilding and Drydock Company for construction of CVA-67. It would be another six months before the keel would be laid (October 22, 1964). CVA-67, now bearing the name JOHN F. KENNEDY, would not join the fleet until late 1968. Symbolic of the crisis over what would perhaps be the last oil-fired carrier, and distinguishing the JOHN F. KENNEDY from other conventional carriers, would be the rakish angle of the stacks. The uptakes for exhaust from the boilers would be angled outboard thirty degrees from vertical. The severe corrosion problem, especially as it affects aircraft aboard (this would be nonexistent on a nuclear carrier), was recognized and dealt with if only in a somewhat improvising manner.

Epilogue

Two more years would pass before the Secretary of Defense would lay before Congress his first recommendation for a nuclear-powered naval surface unit. Testifying before the Joint Committee on Atomic Energy on the question of nonproliferation of nuclear weapons, Secretary McNamara revealed that he had included in his fiscal year 1967 requests a recommendation for authorization and funding of a nuclear-powered attack carrier (CVAN-68). [71] Two days later before the House Armed Services Committee, Mr. McNamara not only spoke of his request for a nuclear-powered carrier, but revealed for the first time that he had abandoned his plan to reduce the force level of attack carriers from fifteen to thirteen. [72] A year earlier, in February 1965, he had told the same committee that "my review of this issue [force level of attack carriers] during the past few months confirms my judgment" that the plan in effect since 1963 to operate thirteen attack carriers is justified. [73] This judgment was at odds with that of the Secretary of the Navy. Mr. Nitze said in the "Posture Hearings" on March 2, 1965, that "fifteen attack carriers are the minimum number required to maintain the level of our present capabilities." [74] This force level had been put forward consistently by the Navy throughout the controversy and was based by the Navy on its assessment of United States commitments into the 1970s. In adopting the force-level figure of fifteen, and in agreeing to the construction of a nuclear-powered attack carrier, the Secretary of Defense did not utilize the Navy justification.

Typically, Mr. McNamara supported his new judgment in his own "effectiveness" terms. It was clear that the World War II ESSEX class CVA's could not be retained in the attack carrier force; they were not able to operate the F-4's, not to mention the projected F-111-B's. Somewhat at odds with his earlier view, Mr. McNamara stated that "large carriers" would be required for the CVA force. The fact that only two reactors would be required for CVAN-68 now made nuclear propulsion cost effective, although the total outlay would probably be greater than that for a four-reactor carrier in fiscal year 1963.

There was a new element in Mr. McNamara's justification of fifteen attack carriers which suggested that a new conflict might be in the offing. The Secretary of Defense proposed that the traditional one-for-one relationship between attack carriers and air wings (carrier air groups) be altered. He submitted a plan whereby the air complement for fifteen carriers would be twelve air wings rather than fifteen. [75] The plan, needless to say, did not originate with the Navy but was forwarded to the secretary from the office of the Assistant Secretary of Defense (Systems Analysis).[76] In their statements to the House Armed Services Committee on April 26, 1966, the Secretary of the Navy and the Chief of Naval Operations conspicuously omitted any reference to the plan.[77] Mr. McNamara felt that "significantly more usable combat power" could be obtained under this plan, although "some change in the present mode of operation" of carriers would be required. "Carriers would normally deploy with less than the maximum complement of aircraft and additional aircraft would be flown to the carriers as needed. In effect, we would be treating the aircraft carrier as a forward floating air base, deploying the aircraft as the situation requires."[78] The Navy was not persuaded that the "forward floating air base" concept was superior to the prevailing concept of an integral, self-sustaining task force. Nor was it persuaded that the Secretary of Defense had properly assessed operating experience on "Yankee" and "Dixie" stations off Vietnam, especially the critical issues of aircraft and pilot requirements in "wartime" circumstances.[79]

There was often acrimonious debate between the Secretary of Defense and the Congress in the two years following the CVA-67 case over the question of major surface unit construction for the Navy. Nuclear escorts for the nuclear-powered carriers were at the center of the continuing controversy, but the overall level of surface unit construction was the basic question. Noting that fleet aging (that is, the number of ships over twenty years old) would reach a peak in 1969, Chairman L. Mendel Rivers of the House Armed Services Committee expressed his concern in March 1965 over "the continued lack of new construction of major surface warships." In October 1965, Secretary McNamara advised Congressman Rivers that there was disagreement within the Navy about the advisability of nuclear propulsion in frigates. On December 1, 1965, the Chief of Naval Operations,

Admiral David L. McDonald, informed Congressman Rivers by letter to the contrary. [80] The Secretary of Defense had concurred in the construction of a nuclear-powered aircraft carrier in his sixth year in office. At the same time he had opened up a new issue on the air complement for an attack carrier and had left the even more far-reaching issue of new surface unit construction in doubt. There was little evidence after five years of a common understanding of sea power; there was evidence of continuing controversy.

Appendix: Chronology of a Decision

1. *February 8, 1962: Admiral George W. Anderson, Chief of Naval Operations, Testimony to House Armed Services Committee.*
   "Perhaps the greatest single achievement in the history of the Navy has been the application of nuclear power first to our submarines and now to surface ships."
   "For obvious reasons I would much prefer to have more nuclear ships in this year's budget [fiscal year 1963] . . . There are, however, two primary reasons why we do not desire *at this time* to proceed too rapidly with the construction of nuclear surface ships. *One of these is a lack of money* . . . The second reason is a desire to observe the performance of the ships we now have in commission and at the same time to afford sufficient time for ultimate reduction in cost and weight of nuclear reactors and an increase in their unit power . . . When that day comes you may rest assured all possible emphasis will be given to the building of [nuclear] surface ships."
2. *February 28, 1962: Hon. Fred Korth, Secretary of the Navy, Testimony to Defense Subcommittee, Senate Appropriations Committee.*
   "We fully recognize the operational benefits to be derived from a nuclear-powered carrier . . . However, I consider it prudent that we limit our present nuclear-powered carriers to one, to afford ourselves time to evaluate this force thoroughly . . . in light of the urgent need for other ships, and in consideration of the factors mentioned, I do not believe that the additional cost of *about one-third to one-half more* to provide nuclear power can be sustained *at this time.*"

3. *February-March-April 1962.*

Shakedown trials of ENTERPRISE.

Joint Committee on Atomic Energy visits ENTERPRISE at Guantanamo Bay, May 31 and April 1; it concluded that "the United States must prosecute vigorously the conversion of the Navy to nuclear propulsion in the surface fleet as well as in the submarine fleet."

House Armed Services Committee adds a DLGN to fiscal year 1963 budget which Department of Defense had not requested. Secretary of Defense cancels the fiscal year 1963 DLGN in fall of 1962 because of difficulties with TYPHON antiair warfare missile system, thus ending the nuclear surface warship construction program. (DLGN TRUXTON, fiscal year 1962, had been changed from oil to nuclear propulsion by House action in May 1961.)

4. *March 30, 1962: Memorandum from Hon. Fred Korth, Secretary of the Navy, to Hon. Roswell Gilpatric, Deputy Secretary of Defense.*

"Navy policy calls positively for movement in the direction of nuclear propulsion . . . the best means at our disposal to reduce costs of these nuclear powered ships is to expand the nuclear shipbuilding effort."

5. *October-November-December 1962.*

Vice Admiral John T. Hayward has command of CVAN-65 ENTERPRISE, in Task Force 135, during Cuban missile crisis and subsequent blockade. (Task Force 135 also included the conventional, Forrestal class carrier INDEPENDENCE.) Admiral Hayward submits his findings to Secretary Korth in a letter of January 2, 1963. See below, 8.

6. *December 18, 1962: Letter from Naval Research Advisory Committee to Hon. Fred Korth, Secretary of the Navy (Signed by NRAC Chairman, D. E. R. Piore, Vice President for Research and Development, International Business Machines Corporation).*

"We would like to urge that all future major combatant surface ships have nuclear power plants . . . Very often detailed analysis confuses the issues in making bold technical decisions . . . we feel that there has been sufficient analysis to indicate the direction of future work."

7. *December 18, 1962.*

Members of the Atomic Energy Commission visit CVAN-65 ENTERPRISE at sea. Findings are reflected in a letter from Chairman of AEC, Mr. Glenn Seaborg, to Secretary of Defense dated January 7, 1963. See below, 9.

8. *January 2, 1963: Letter from Vice Admiral John T. Hayward, Commander of Task Force 135, to Hon. Fred Korth, Secretary of the Navy.*

"My experience in ENTERPRISE to date has convinced me more than ever that the military advantages of nuclear propulsion in surface combatant ships more than outweigh their extra cost . . . ENTERPRISE outperforms every carrier in the fleet . . . In Washington these often cited advantages of nuclear propulsion seem to get lost in a shuffle of paper—off Cuba they were real . . . I have learned, often through bitter experience, that real improvements in our hardware are only made through building and evaluating in service . . . my experience tells me that nuclear propulsion offers the Navy tremendous military advantages that will be sorely needed in the years ahead . . . I am deeply disturbed that we are not exploiting to the fullest the technological advantage we hold in nuclear propulsion . . . I do not believe you can weigh victory or defeat on a scale of dollars and cents—yet the margin between victory and defeat in future naval engagements may well depend on the availability of nuclear-powered ships." See below, 10.

9. *January 7, 1963: Letter from Mr. Glenn T. Seaborg, Chairman, Atomic Energy Commission, to Mr. Robert McNamara, Secretary of Defense.*

"The Commission has been working for more than 3 years on the design and development of a reactor suitable for powering a *four-reactor* carrier . . . the proposed reactor represents *a significant advance in technology* . . . further, our studies indicate that the cost of buying and installing four of the higher powered reactor plants is expected to be about *one-third less* than the cost of the eight reactor plants on ENTERPRISE . . . we believe the Commission's development program has reached a point where an overall appraisal of the future of nuclear propulsion plants for surface warships is needed for us to be able to determine the level and scale of effort of the Commission's program in the next few years . . . we would like to raise the question whether it is too late to reconsider this decision [the decision to build CVA-67 with conventional power] . . . our own experience in this field indicates that the program has reached a stage of maturity and of promise that would justify consideration by the Department [of Defense] of *a significant increase in the application of nuclear power to the surface fleet* in its shipbuilding program in the years immediately ahead."

10. *January 23, 1963: Memorandum from the Secretary of the*

Navy (Fred Korth) to Secretary of Defense (Robert McNamara).
"Dr. Seaborg's letter to you of January 7 . . . suggested an overall
appraisal of the future of nuclear propulsion for surface warships
. . . additionally, it raised the question of whether it is too late to
reconsider the decision to build CVA-67 . . . as a conventionally
fueled ship . . . it is certainly appropriate that we reappraise our
position and plans in the field . . . as a result of my review of all
pertinent considerations, as highlighted by Dr. Seaborg's letter, I
conclude that the substitution of an improved four-reactor nuclear
propulsion plant for the oil-fired plant now programmed for
CVA-67 is *both feasible and desirable* . . . I suggest therefore your
consideration *as a matter of urgency.*"

11. *February 2, 1963: Mr. McNamara Replies to Mr. Seaborg's Letter
of January 7.*
"This is to advise you that we are reconsidering our decision to
build CVA-67 as a conventionally fueled ship . . . It is being pursued
as *a matter of urgency.*" (There was no reference to an overall
appraisal of the future of nuclear propulsion for surface warships.)

12. *February 22, 1963: Mr. McNamara Replies to Mr. Korth's Memorandum of January 23.*
(This is a turning point. Here Mr. McNamara shifts ground from
the question of appropriate propulsion for CVA-67 to the question
of nuclear power in the Navy's future, demanding a comprehensive,
quantitative study of the latter as a condition for determining the
former.)
"I do not feel that the subject of nuclear propulsion for surface
warships has yet been explored sufficiently to permit a rational
decision [on nuclear propulsion for CVA-67] . . . I am sure you realize that they [Navy arguments for nuclear propulsion in CVA-67]
*depend upon the assumption that the future Navy will, indeed,
make full use of nuclear power.* It is precisely this question which
lies at the heart of the matter; far more so than the question of
whether CVA-67 itself should or should not be nuclear powered.
Accordingly, *I should like you to undertake a comprehensive, quantitative study of this matter* . . . As a general guide, I am interested
in achieving the most efficient possible naval forces, *defining efficiency as achieving the most beneficial military results for a given
expenditure* . . . I am reserving decision on the question of nuclear
propulsion for CVA-67."

13. *April 4, 1963: Memorandum from Secretary of the Navy (Korth)
Responding to the Secretary of Defense's Request Contained in His
Memorandum of February 22, 1963.*

"You stated that the assumption the future Navy will make full use of nuclear power lies at the heart of the matter of whether we should change the CVA-67 to nuclear propulsion. I concur . . . I have concluded that nuclear propulsion does permit a significant increase in the beneficial military results for a given expenditure and that we must exploit and take maximum advantage of it . . . we have come to the conclusion that all new major warships should be nuclear powered . . . I believe that we have sufficiently resolved those major questions you have raised . . . I commend the decision on CVA-67 to your consideration as a matter of urgency."

14. *April 20, 1963: Secretary of Defense Replies to "First Navy Study" Contained in the Secretary of the Navy's Memorandum of April 4, 1963.*

(This memo is important in that the Secretary of Defense spells out much of what he means by cost-effectiveness analysis especially as it applies to the comparative merits of nuclear and conventional propulsion for surface warships.)

"Your memorandum does not provide me with the information I need in order to reach a decision in this important matter. Specifically, my question concerning the implications of nuclear power for force size has not been answered . . . you have failed to identify the magnitude of the increase in effectiveness or the possible reduction in force . . . I realize it is difficult to quantify exactly the increase in effectiveness associated with nuclear propulsion, but I would like you and the Chief of Naval Operations to indicate to me the nuclear powered force which, in your judgment, would be equivalent in effectiveness to a conventional force. Similarly, my question on the implications of nuclear power for the composition of task forces has not been answered . . . while I realize that there are many issues involved here which are not subject to rigorous quantitative analysis, a systematic exposition of those issues which are quantifiable is necessary if I am to appreciate fully your position. Let me cite two issues raised in my mind by your memorandum. First, I have been concerned for some time that the steadily increasing size of escort ships may be adding a disproportionate share to the cost of each attack aircraft sortie delivered from our carriers, in comparison with alternative means . . . The second issue also involved your comparisons of nuclear-powered and conventional task force costs . . . I should like to know the basis for this assumption (re escort differentials in the two task forces), and the reason why only the replenishment ships associated with the conventional task force require the expensive protection of DDG's."

The Secretary of Defense then went on to suggest cost-effectiveness criteria by which the Secretary of the Navy was to be guided in his further studies and asked the Navy to work with his Office of Systems Analysis in pursuing these studies.

15. *September 26, 1963: Memorandum from Secretary of the Navy (Korth) to Secretary of Defense (McNamara) Forwarding "Second Navy Study" Done under the Direction of Rear Admiral T. F. Connolly, Director, Strike Warfare Division, Office of Naval Operations.*

This memorandum stipulates a comprehensive list of advantages enjoyed by a nuclear surface warship over a conventional surface ship and states that five nuclear task forces are the equal of or superior to six conventional task forces. (Note: In his testimony Admiral Connolly points out that the real question is comparing a force level of fifteen attack carriers, only one of which is nuclear, with a fourteen-ship level of which only eight are conventional and six are nuclear—in this case there is no question of the superiority of the latter.) It points out further that the lifetime cost differential of a nuclear and a conventional task force is of the order of 3 percent. The memorandum concludes by noting again that CVA-67 would be the only nuclear ship authorized since 1961 and that the next opportunity to build a CVAN would be years ahead. The Secretary of Defense rejected the memorandum. In response to the Navy's answer to his first question, namely that five nuclear task forces were superior to six conventional task forces, the Secretary of Defense stated, "I am absolutely certain of one thing, that the six conventional task forces are superior to the five nuclear task forces." See below, 17.

16. *October 9, 1963: Letter from Senator John O. Pastore, Chairman, Joint Committee on Atomic Energy, to Secretary of Defense (McNamara).*

Senator Pastore notes that in response to a letter he had addressed to the Secretary of Defense on March 1, 1963, concerning "the slow progress in the application of nuclear power for the propulsion of naval surface vessels," the Director of Defense Research and Engineering (Mr. Harold Brown) had replied to the effect that the matter was being reexamined on a priority basis and that the Joint Committee "would be advised of the results in the near future." Senator Pastore then notes that the only information he has received has been from the press. The Chairman of the Joint Committee specifically asks the Secretary of Defense to respond to a story by Jack Raymond of *The New York Times* (September 29,

1963) in which it is reported that the Secretary of Defense decided not to put nuclear propulsion in CVA-67. Senator Pastore asks for copies of such studies as have been made on the question and informs the Secretary of Defense of impending hearings before the Joint Committee on Atomic Energy on nuclear propulsion for naval surface vessels.

17. *October 9, 1963: Memorandum from Secretary of Defense (McNamara) in Reply to the Secretary of the Navy's Memorandum of September 26, 1963.*

(Note that this memo from the Secretary of Defense to the Secretary of the Navy is dated the same day as Senator Pastore's letter to the Secretary of Defense, asking whether Mr. Raymond's story in *The New York Times* of September 29, 1963, is correct.) "My original intent in requesting a comprehensive study of nuclear propulsion was to expand the particular issue of the fiscal year 1963 carrier to a general policy issue . . . on the basis of the analysis to date, I am not convinced that a net advantage is in prospect. While it is clear that nuclear propulsion would result in some desirable characteristics, the increased cost (particularly in ship construction) remains a serious disadvantage . . . Considering the state of the legislative calendar and the previously expressed attitudes on the subject of certain key congressional leaders, it is doubtful, to say the least, that congressional approval of a shift to nuclear propulsion for the fiscal year 1963 carrier would be either swift or sure. As a result, I believe that the fiscal year 1963 carrrier should proceed on the conventionally powered basis as authorized by the Congress. I would like you to take the proper steps to proceed with the construction as soon as possible."

18. *October 10, 1963: Memorandum from the Secretary of the Navy (Korth) Replying to the Memorandum of October 9, 1963 from the Secretary of Defense.* (Note the lapse of only one day.)

"I was surprised to receive your memorandum of October 9 in which you asked me to take the proper steps to proceed with construction of the fiscal year 1963 carrier with conventional power rather than nuclear power . . . I earnestly request that you reconsider the decison on the method of propulsion for the fiscal year 1963 carrier . . . based on the shipbuilding program you have proposed there will not be another opportunity to build a nuclear surface ship for several years."

19. *October 11, 1963: Letter from Deputy Secretary of Defense (Gilpatric) to Senator John O. Pastore, Chairman, Joint Committee on Atomic Energy.*

(Note that just two days after the Secretary of Defense has directed the Secretary of the Navy to proceed with construction of CVA-67 on a conventional basis, the Deputy Secretary of Defense tells the Chairman of the Joint Committee on Atomic Energy that the final decision has not yet been made.)

"Contrary to reports in the press, final decision with respect to the type of propulsion to be installed in the aircraft carrier authorized by Congress in fiscal year 1963 has not yet been made. As soon as we are in a position to do so, we will inform you of our action with respect to this matter."

20. *October 22, 1963: Letter from Senator John O. Pastore, Chairman, Joint Committee on Atomic Energy, to Director of Defense Research and Engineering (Mr. Harold Brown).*

Senator Pastore states his pleasure that press reports to the effect that CVA-67 is to have conventional power are incorrect. He informs the Department of Defense of hearing dates and again requests that studies he asked for two weeks previous be forwarded to him.

21. *October 25, 1963: Memorandum from Secretary of Defense (McNamara) to Secretary of the Navy (Korth) Pursuant to the Latter's Request That the Secretary of Defense Reconsider His Decision of October 9, 1963.*

(This "final" statement from the Secretary of Defense is significant in that it contains points which were found to be fallacious in subsequent hearings before the Joint Committee on Atomic Energy.)

"I have concluded that steps should be taken immediately to initiate construction of the conventionally powered aircraft carrier authorized by the Congress in fiscal year 1963 . . . the real choice we face is not between a given number of conventional ships for one sum of money and the same number of nuclear ships for a larger sum. The choice is between a given number of conventional ships and a smaller number of nuclear ships at the same total cost."

(The Joint Committee on Atomic Energy rejected this statement.) The Secretary of Defense then states that the Navy judgment that five nuclear task forces are as good as six conventional task forces is "not generally valid." His references to comparative transit times and deployment with amphibious forces as well as the "logistics tail" are sharply refuted in testimony before the Joint Committee.

22. *October-November 1963: Hearings before the Joint Committee on Atomic Energy on Naval Nuclear Propulsion Program.*

In its report issued in December 1963, the Joint Committee

recommended that "the decision to install conventional propulsion in the new aircraft carrier, CVA-67, should be set aside and plans made to install nuclear propulsion in this ship." The Joint Committee hearings, owing largely to Senators Pastore and Jackson, represent a significant "intervention" by the Congress. It is also significant that as compelling as the case for nuclear propulsion was, the congressional effort was unavailing.

23. *February 26, 1964: Letter from Senator Henry M. Jackson to Rear Admiral T. F. Connolly.*

Subsequent to the Joint Committee on Atomic Energy hearings, Senator Henry M. Jackson, Chairman of the Military Applications Subcommittee of the Joint Committee, asked the Navy for additional information on the comparative merits of nuclear and conventional carriers especially with respect to the issue of logistic support required by each.

24. *March 5, 1964: Admiral Connolly Replies to Senator Jackson.*

The Navy responded with a detailed comparison of a four-reactor attack carrier and a conventionally powered vessel. It did not restate "the general advantages of the nuclear warships." In summary the Navy reported that "a nuclear CVAN-67 is designed to carry ammunition, aircraft fuel, and propulsion fuel for conventional escorts sufficient to deliver *at least 60% more* airstrikes than a conventional CVA-67 before replenishing." For situations requiring extended transits, the relative capabilities of the nuclear carrier are still greater.

25. *March 6, 1964.*

Admiral Hyman C. Rickover, in an appearance before the Defense Subcommittee of the House Appropriations Committee, asks, "Is it still possible for Congress to do anything about the nuclear powered carrier? . . . Actually the case is even stronger now that further study has been done since the Joint Committee considered this."

26. *April 17, 1964.*

House Committee on Appropriations, "in the absence of a request from the Department of Defense," does not recommend funds for nuclear propulsion of fiscal year 1963 aircraft carrier (CVA-67).

27. *April 30, 1964.*

Contract let to Newport News Shipbuilding and Drydock Company for construction of conventionally powered attack carrier (CVA–67). More than two years had elapsed from the time of authorization. Ship would not join the fleet until 1968-69.

28. *June 18, 1964.*
    President Johnson authorizes that CVA-67 be named JOHN F. KENNEDY. Suggests that the tentatively scheduled fiscal year 1967 carrier will have a two-reactor nuclear power plant.
29. *February 18, 1965.*
    The Secretary of Defense tells House Armed Services Committee that the odds are three to one in favor of his recommending a two-reactor carrier in 1966 (fiscal year 1967 budget).
30. *March 24, 1965.*
    Chairman Rivers of the House Armed Services Committee inquires of the Secretary of Defense concerning "the continued lack of new construction of major surface warships."
31. *April 5, 1965.*
    The Secretary of Defense's reply to Rivers' letter is classified.
32. *April 27, 1965.*
    Chairman Rivers responds to the Secretary of Defense's letter of April 5, 1965. He states that while there may be a two-reactor carrier in fiscal year 1967, no nuclear-powered surface ships are programmed for the next five years.
33. *May 8, 1965.*
    The Secretary of Defense declares he is still reserving decision on nuclear-powered surface units.
34. *July 26, 1965.*
    Preliminary design contract for a two-reactor carrier (CVAN-68) is let to Newport News Shipbuilding and Drydock Company. Department of Defense announces no commitment is involved.
35. *March 7, 1966.*
    Secretary of Defense McNamara tells Joint Committee on Atomic Energy that he is recommending to Congress that the fiscal year 1967 carrier (CVAN-68) be authorized and funded for nuclear propulsion. This is his first such recommendation.

Notes

Notes to Introduction

1. Samuel P. Huntington could write a decade ago that "no one role for the Secretary and no one pattern of civil-military relations has yet emerged as dominant . . . in the end, accumulated practice rather than statutory enactment will determine the place of the Secretary." This remains true today and prompts the present study of "accumulated practice." See Huntington, *The Soldier and the State: The Theory and Politics of Civil-Military Relations* (Cambridge, 1957), p. 441.

2. These terms are preferred to "active" and "passive" as descriptive of role concepts. While the latter have had some currency, especially since the Rockefeller Committee Report of 1953, it is the conclusion of the author that they do not represent adequately the distinction that has arisen in the practice of the Secretaries of Defense.

3. Demetrios Caraley, *The Politics of Military Unification* (New York, 1966). In this excellent study, Professor Caraley finds on the basis of his examination of the unification conflict that "There is no good reason to believe that any particular single actor who might be given dominant control over either the general policy-making process or the policy-making process within the military establishment could anticipate the future better than the larger number who become involved in a more pluralistic, conflict-producing system, nor is there any guarantee that the same actor would conceive of the most correct solution in every respect . . . In the last analysis the formulation and adoption of governmental policies with the proper combination of responsiveness to public interests, non-oppressiveness to private

interests, and correctness as judged by later events will depend not nearly so much on the form of the policy-making process as on the wisdom, the courage, and the good judgment of the individual officials whom the American public chooses to operate it" (p. 289).
4. Karl Mannheim, *Ideology and Utopia* (London, 1936), p. 105.

Notes to Chapter 1

1. Samuel P. Huntington, *The Soldier and the State: The Theory and Politics of Civil-Military Relations* (Cambridge, 1957), pp. 336-337, 429-430; John C. Ries, *The Management of Defense: Organization and Control of the United States Armed Services* (Baltimore, 1964), pp. 3-20; Paul Y. Hammond, *Organizing for Defense* (New York, 1961), pp. 186-226; *Hearings,* before House Select Committee on Postwar Military Policy on Proposal to Establish a Single Department of the Armed Forces, 78th Congress, 2nd Session (1944); *Report,* of House Select Committee (issued with the *Hearings*); *Hearings,* before Senate Committee on Military Affairs on a Single Department of National Defense, 79th Congress, 1st Session (1945); *Hearings,* before Senate Committee on Naval Affairs, 79th Congress, 1st Session (1945).
2. Ries, *The Management of Defense,* p. 37.
3. *Ibid.,* p. 65.
4. Robert G. Albion and Robert H. Connery, *Forrestal and the Navy* (New York, 1962), pp. 250, 257, 264.
5. *Ibid.,* pp. 262-263; Walter Millis, ed., *The Forrestal Diaries* (New York, 1951), pp. 87, 164.
6. *Report,* by Ferdinand Eberstadt to Secretary of the Navy Forrestal on Unification of the War and Navy Departments and Postwar Organization for National Security, Senate Committee on National Affairs, 79th Congress, 1st Session (1945); Ries, *The Management of Defense,* pp. 55ff.; Albion and Connery, *Forrestal and the Navy,* pp. 263-266.
7. *Forrestal and the Navy,* pp. 259, 280; also personal conversation with Professor Connery.
8. Ries, *The Management of Defense,* pp. 64-65; Albion and Connery, *Forrestal and the Navy,* p. 281.
9. Quoted by Albion and Connery, *Forrestal and the Navy,* pp. 274-275.

10. *Ibid.*, pp. 277, 273-274; Millis, *The Forrestal Diaries*, pp. 223-224; *Hearings*, before Senate Committee on Naval Affairs, 79th Congress, 1st Session (1945).
11. Millis, *The Forrestal Diaries*, p. 228; Albion and Connery, *Forrestal and the Navy*, pp. 185-186, 231, 272.
12. Louis W. Koenig, *The Truman Administration* (New York, 1956), p. 363; Albion and Connery, *Forrestal and the Navy*, pp. 261, 267, 273; Harry S. Truman, *Memoirs* (2 vols., New York, 1955-1956).
13. Quoted by Albion and Connery, *Forrestal and the Navy*, p. 280; *Hearings*, before Senate Committee on Armed Services on S. 758, A Bill to Promote the National Security by Providing for a National Defense Establishment, 80th Congress, 1st Session (1947), pp. 22-26.
14. Quoted by Ries, *The Management of Defense*, p. 103
15. *Ibid.*, p. 106; Albion and Connery, *Forrestal and the Navy*, Ch. 9 especially.
16. Millis, *The Forrestal Diaries*, pp. 152, 245. Millis has an apt summation: "If in the end Forrestal was largely the winner in the unification fight, it was because he had thought more deeply . . . because he had looked at the real and central problems involved rather than accepted quick solutions which under the test of time and events could not stand" (p. 162).
17. *Ibid.*, p. 301.
18. *Ibid.*; Albion and Connery, *Forrestal and the Navy*, pp. 280-281.
19. Quoted by Arnold A. Rogow, *James Forrestal, A Study of Personality, Politics, and Policy* (New York, 1963), p. 293; Joseph E. McLean, *The Public Service and University Education* (Princeton, 1949), pp. 513-514.
20. There is ample literature on Forrestal's budget difficulties for both fiscal year 1949 and fiscal year 1950. See Millis, *Forrestal Diaries*, pp. 430-439, 462-469, 412-421, 475-478, 499-500, 502-506; Huntington, *The Soldier and the State*, pp. 445-447; Warren R. Schilling, "The Politics of National Defense: Fiscal 1950," in Warren R. Schilling, Paul Y. Hammond, and Glenn H. Snyder, *Strategy, Politics and Defense Budgets* (New York, 1962), pp. 1-266; Ries, *The Management of Defense*, pp. 114-118; Hammond, *Organizing for Defense*, pp. 213ff.; and Rogow, *James Forrestal*, pp. 288-303.
21. National Military Establishment, *First Report of the Secretary of Defense* (Washington, 1948).

22. Commission on Organization of the Executive Branch of Government, *Task Force Report on National Security Organization* (Washington, 1949).
23. *Hearings*, before the Subcommittee on National Policy Machinery of the Senate Committee on Government Operations, Organizing for National Security, 87th Congress, 1st Session (1961), Vol. I, p. 11.
24. Huntington, *The Soldier and the State*, p. 280; Rogow, *James Forrestal*, pp. 1-6, 311.
25. For the prior determination of national political goals as a guide to military policy and planning, see *Hearings*, Subcommittee on National Policy Machinery (1961), Vol. I, pp. 16ff. For Lovett's views about the professional military, see Robert A. Lovett, "Role of the Military Services in Government" (Memorandum for Special Preparedness Subcommittee of the Senate Committee on Armed Services), in *Selected Papers*, compiled by the Subcommittee on National Security Staffing and Operations, Senate Committee on Government Operations, 87th Congress, 2nd Session (1962), pp. 137-143; Robert A. Lovett, "Address," August 10, 1960, in *Selected Readings*, compiled by the Subcommittee on National Security and International Operations, Senate Committee on Government Operations, Committee Print, 89th Congress, 1st Session (1965), pp. 27-35; Robert A. Lovett, "Address," May 2, 1964, in *Hearings*, before the Subcommittee on National Security Staffing and Operations, Senate Committee on Government Operations, 88th Congress, 2nd Session (1964), Appendix, pp. 585-587.
26. *Hearings*, Subcommittee on National Policy Machinery (1961), Vol. I, p. 43; Huntington, *The Soldier and the State*, p. 443.
27. Edward B. Lockett, "Again the Marshall-Lovett Team," *New York Times*, October 29, 1950.
28. *Hearings*, Subcommittee on National Policy Machinery (1961), Vol. I, pp. 784-785.
29. *Ibid.*, Vol. I, p. 16.
30. *Ibid.*, Vol. I, pp. 17, 15; Huntington, *The Soldier and the State*, pp. 443, 447-448.
31. *Hearings*, Subcommittee on National Policy Machinery (1961), Vol. I, pp. 17, 42; Albion and Connery, *Forrestal and the Navy*, p. 264 (re the similarity of Lovett's view to that of the Eberstadt Report).
32. Lockett, "Again the Marshall-Lovett Team."
33. Ries, *The Management of Defense*, pp. 148-152, 155, 157. Lovett's

concept of the Joint Chiefs of Staff would seem to be sufficiently clear. It is a strange logic that traces the removal of the JCS from the command line in 1953 (restored in 1958) to him. As opposed to Lovett's testimony before the Jackson Subcommittee (Subcommittee on National Policy Machinery) in February 1960 (which was based largely on notes dating from 1952), Walter Millis writes that Lovett "intimated" the JCS should become purely a planning staff. See Walter Millis, *Arms and the State* (New York, 1951), p. 370. The Rockefeller Committee Report in 1953 does not support this intimation, and it is specifically rejected by the counsel to the committee, H. Struve Hensel. See Senate Committee on Armed Services, *Report of the Rockefeller Committee: Department of Defense Organization,* Committee Print, 83rd Congress, 1st Session (1953), p. v., and H. Struve Hensel, "Changes Inside the Pentagon," *Harvard Business Review,* XXXII (January-February 1954), 105; see also Hammond, *Organizing for Defense,* pp. 259-261, and Huntington, *The Soldier and the State,* pp. 437-438, 440, 443.

34. Robert A. Lovett, letter to the President, November 18, 1952; *Army Navy Air Force Journal,* January 10, 1953, pp. 542-543.
35. Huntington, *The Soldier and the State,* p. 450.
36. *Hearings,* Subcommittee on National Policy Machinery (1961), Vol. I, p. 14.
37. Jack Raymond, "A Sailor for the Top Defense Job," *New York Times,* November 29, 1959. A veteran observer of the Pentagon, C. J. V. Murphy, wrote that Gates was "in the tradition of General George Marshall and Robert Lovett." Gates' most marked attributes," he continued, "are a reasonableness in outlook, diligence, a rare sense of duty, and (in contrast with some businessmen who have been drafted for the Pentagon) a high respect for the competence of the military." "Is the Defense Budget Big Enough? " *Fortune,* LX (November 1959), 145-146. Nearly a decade later, a career Navy officer would say, "Tom Gates was the best all-around Secretary we've had since Forrestal." *U.S. News and World Report* (July 25, 1966), p. 35. For a summary of the level of experience of the "Gates Team" in the Department of Defense, see Gene M. Lyons, "The New Civil-Military Relations," *The American Political Science Review,* LV (March 1961), 57n.
38. *Hearings,* Subcommittee on National Policy Machinery (1961), Vol. I, p. 734. Gates suggested to the committee that "there is growing recognition that people who serve in Congress and serve in

statutory appointee positions dealing with important questions, particularly defense and foreign policy, are beginning to earn a more important position in the way of life of the United States" (p. 741). See also *Hearings,* before House Committee on Government Operations on Reorganization Plan No. 6 of 1953, Department of Defense, 83rd Congress, 1st Session (1953), p. 2.

39. *Hearings,* Subcommittee on National Policy Machinery (1961), Vol. I, pp. 746-748, 763-764.

40. *Hearings,* before the Subcommittee of the House Committee on Appropriations on Department of Defense Appropriations for 1961, 86th Congress, 2nd Session (1960), Part I, pp. 34-35. It should be noted that General Nathan Twining, Chairman of the Joint Chiefs of Staff, concurred with Secretary Gates in his rejection of a single chief.

41. *Hearings,* House Defense Subcommittee (1960), Part I, pp. 37-38.

42. *Selected Papers,* Subcommittee on National Security Staffing and Operations (1962), p. 145; *Hearings,* Subcommittee on National Policy Machinery (1961), Vol. I, p. 730.

43. *Hearings,* Subcommittee on National Policy Machinery (1961), Vol. I, p. 735.

44. *Hearings,* House Defense Subcommittee (1960), Part I, p. 122; *Hearings,* Subcommittee on National Policy Machinery (1961), Vol. I, p. 753.

45. *Hearings,* House Defense Subcommittee (1960), Part I, p. 35.

46. *Hearings,* Subcommittee on National Policy Machinery (1961), Vol. I, p. 737. Emphasis supplied.

47. *Hearings,* House Defense Subcommittee (1960), Part I, p. 17.

48. *Hearings,* Subcommittee on National Policy Machinery (1961), Vol. I, p. 752. Wilfred J. McNeil, Department of Defense Comptroller from 1949 to 1959, makes precisely the same point about the rigidity of the functional budget; *ibid.,* Vol. I, p. 1066. For a contrary view, see General Maxwell Taylor's testimony before the same subcommittee (also known as the Jackson Subcommittee), Vol. I, pp. 769-770, 780ff., and Maxwell Taylor, *The Uncertain Trumpet* (New York, 1959), pp. 162-164. For an extended discussion, see Chapter II.

49. Dwight D. Eisenhower, *The White House Years,* Vol. I: *Mandate for Change, 1953-1956* (New York, 1963), pp. 445-458. See his five basic considerations that provided "logical guidelines for designing and employing a security establishment" (pp. 446-447). Walter Millis found Eisenhower in an excellent position to "influence the Joint Chiefs as a civilian" and to "restore

non-military considerations to a greater authority"; *Arms and the State*, p. 376. See also Sherman Adams, *Firsthand Report— The Story of the Eisenhower Administration* (New York, 1961), pp. 154-155, 396ff.

50. General Robert Cutler, Special Assistant to President Eisenhower for National Security Affairs for four years, relates that the President participated vigorously in 90 percent of the National Security Council meetings. See *Hearings*, Subcommittee on National Policy Machinery (1961), Vol. I, p. 588. Sherman Adams, Special Assistant to the President, has written that Mr. Eisenhower took NSC discussions "more seriously than almost any other duty of his office"; *Firsthand Report*, p. 412. See also Glenn M. Snyder, "The New Look of 1953," in Schilling, Hammond, and Snyder, *Strategy, Politics and Defense Budgets*, pp. 400-410, for a discussion of stabilized but reduced budgets.

51. *Report of the Rockefeller Committee: Department of Defense Organization* (1953), p. v.; Senate Committee on Armed Services, *Reorganization Plan No. 6 of 1953 Relating to the Department of Defense*, 83rd Congress, 1st Session (1953).

52. Hensel, "Changes Inside the Pentagon," p. 106; Hammond, *Organizing for Defense*, p. 303. For Mr. Rockefeller's testimony on this point, see *Hearings*, before House Committee on Government Operations on Reorganization Plan No. 6 of 1953, Department of Defense, 83rd Congress, 1st Session (1953), pp. 148-156.

53. Hammond, *Organizing for Defense*, pp. 312, 314; Snyder, in Schilling, Hammond, and Snyder, *Strategy, Politics and Defense Budgets*, pp. 426ff.

54. C. J. V. Murphy, "Strategy Overtakes Mr. Wilson," *Fortune*, XLIX (January 1954), 80-81; Duncan Norton-Taylor, "The Wilson Pentagon," *Fortune*, L (December 1954), 96ff.; Huntington, *The Soldier and the State*, pp. 393-394; John McDonald, "The Businessman in Government," *Fortune*, L (July 1954); Emmet J. Hughes, *The Ordeal of Power* (New York, 1962), pp. 64-68.

55. C. J. V. Murphy, "The Embattled McElroy," *Fortune*, LIX (April 1959), 148; Schilling, Hammond, and Snyder, *Strategy, Politics and Defense Budgets*, pp. 439-440.

56. *Firsthand Report*, pp. 402-403; see also Norton-Taylor, "The Wilson Pentagon," p. 96. Generals Gavin and Ridgway write bitterly of Secretary Wilson; see James Gavin, *War and Peace in the Space Age* (New York, 1958), pp. 154-157, and Matthew B. Ridgway, *Soldier: The Memoir of Matthew B. Ridgway* (New York, 1956), pp. 272, 283, 287-294, 323-332.

57. *Hearings,* Subcommittee on National Policy Machinery (1961), Vol. I, p. 588.
58. Eisenhower, *White House Years,* Vol. I, p. 447.
59. *Ibid.,* Vol. I, p. 448.
60. *Hearings,* Subcommittee on National Policy Machinery (1961), Vol. I, p. 668; Millis, *Arms and the State,* pp. 375ff.; Taylor, *The Uncertain Trumpet,* pp. 108ff.; Eisenhower, *White House Years,* Vol. I, pp. 451-455; Schilling, Hammond, and Snyder, *Strategy, Politics and Defense Budgets,* pp. 252-254.
61. Eisenhower, *White House Years,* Vol. I, p. 455.
62. The Rockefeller Panel reports are collected in *Prospect for America* (New York, 1961). For the 1958 report, see Report II, "International Security: The Military Aspect," especially Part VI, "Defense Organization," pp. 118-126, 121.
63. Hammond, *Organizing for Defense,* pp. 321-353.
64. Murphy, "Is the Defense Budget Big Enough?" p. 146; Walter Lippmann, writing at the time of the transition from Wilson to McElroy, was plaintive: "Secretaries come and go. They are chosen from lists of politically available men. They come from banking, from law, from professional politics, from the automobile business and the soap business. How does a man who has spent the first fifty years of his life far away from strategic problems go into the Pentagon, hang up his hat, sit down at the Secretary's desk, and make the decisions which he is supposed to make?" *New York Herald Tribune,* May 8, 1958, quoted by Gavin, *War and Peace in the Space Age,* pp. 258-259.
65. Murphy, "The Embattled McElroy," p. 150. Secretary Gates would have to "explain" to Congress early in 1960 that his predecessor had made a somewhat different analysis of Soviet missile strength than he was now making. *Hearings,* House Defense Subcommittee (1960), Part I, pp. 23-24.
66. See *Hearings,* before the Preparedness Subcommittee of the Senate Committee on Armed Services, Inquiry into Satellite and Missile Programs, 85th Congress, 2nd Session (1958), *passim.*
67. "Special Message to the Congress on Reorganization of the Defense Establishment," *Public Papers of the Presidents: Dwight D. Eisenhower,* VII (April 1958), 274-290. See also, *Communication from the President of the United States Transmitting a Draft of Legislation,* House Committee on Armed Services, 85th Congress, 2nd Session (1958).
68. Eisenhower, "Special Message to the Congress," pp. 294-305. Adams confirms that the President "worked hard on the

reorganization plan himself," and that he "drafted himself, almost word for word, the legislation he wanted enacted." In addition to Mr. Rockefeller, Mr. Charles A. Coolidge was of particular assistance. See *Firsthand Report*, p. 418.

69. *Hearings*, before House Committee on the Armed Services, Reorganization of the Department of Defense, 85th Congress, 2nd Session (1958); *Report*, House Committee on the Armed Services, Department of Defense Reorganization Act of 1958, 85th Congress, 2nd Session (1958), pp. 30-36. Again, Adams relates that after the Symington air power hearings and the "extra" $900 millions voted by Congress for B-52's, the President became convinced that the best device for maintaining policy guidelines was to put the entire defense budget at the disposition of the Secretary of Defense. Then, too, buttressed by the performance of Admiral Radford as JCS Chairman, the President was altogether persuaded of the validity of a single chief supported by an advisory council of officers. See *Firsthand Report*, pp. 404-405. These "private views" of the President were not sent up to Congress in bill form; however, see Nelson Rockefeller's testimony before the Jackson Subcommittee below.

70. Ries, *The Management of Defense*, p. 187; *Report*, House Committee on the Armed Services (1958), pp. 30-36.

71. *Hearings*, House Committee on the Armed Services (1958), *passim; Hearings*, Subcommittee on National Policy Machinery (1961), Vol. I, *passim*. Adams is critical of McElroy's inept testimony which was due, he thought, to the fact that McElroy did not share Eisenhower's "spirited dedication to the reorganization plan." See *Firsthand Report*, pp. 418-419; see also Hughes, *The Ordeal of Power*, p. 226.

72. Ries, *The Management of Defense*, pp. 183ff.

73. *Ibid.*, p. 188.

74. See *Hearings*, Subcommittee on National Policy Machinery (1961), Vol. I, p. 946. Compare the Rockefeller Panel reports, *Prospect for America*, pp. 118-126; See also Schilling, Hammond, and Snyder, *Strategy, Politics and Defense Budgets*, pp. 224, 228.

75. *Hearings*, Subcommittee on National Policy Machinery (1961), Vol. I, pp. 974-975.

76. *Ibid.*, Vol. I, pp. 768ff., 780-782; Taylor, *The Uncertain Trumpet*, pp. 175ff.

77. *Hearings*, Subcommittee on National Policy Machinery (1961), Vol. I, pp. 675, 671.

78. *Ibid.*, Vol. I, pp. 974, 982.
79. Huntington, *The Soldier and the State*, pp. 56ff. and 352.

Notes to Chapter 2

1. *New York Times,* December 6, 1960, p. 30. An avowed admirer of Symington, who chaired this committee, Eugene M. Zuckert declared upon his resignation as Secretary of the Air Force that both he and Deputy Secretary of Defense Roswell L. Gilpatric (who had been a member of the Symington Committee) felt that the committee "had gone too far" in its quest for unification. See Eugene M. Zuckert, "The Service Secretary: Has He a Useful Role? " *Foreign Affairs,* XLIV (April 1966), 462-463, 477.
2. *Hearings,* before the Subcommittee on National Policy Machinery, Senate Committee on Government Operations, 86th Congress, 2nd Session (1961), Vol. I, pp. 1190-1192; Charles J. Hitch, *Decision-Making for Defense* (Berkeley, 1965), pp. 18, 27; H. Struve Hensel, "Changes Inside the Pentagon," *Harvard Business Review,* XXXII (January-February 1954), 108.
3. The basic academic source of Mr. McNamara's thought would be Herbert A. Simon, *Administrative Behavior,* 2nd ed. (New York, 1965), pp. 222ff. Daniel Seligman makes a perceptive observation about the "logic" of Mr. McNamara: "Anyone who has read . . . the transcripts of his long and continuously brilliant appearances before House and Senate committees, cannot fail to be struck by one recurrent note—his insistence on restating questions put to him so they make more sense [to him]. It is clear that the logic of his method requires McNamara to play a much more ambitious role than merely implementing other people's policies. He must also help to structure the questions being debated, make recommendations about the answers, and support his recommendation with a wealth of factual detail." See "McNamara's Management Revolution," *Fortune,* LXXII (July 1965), 250.
4. Robert S. McNamara, "McNamara Defines His Job," *New York Times Magazine* (April 26, 1964), p. 108.
5. *Ibid.* Emphasis supplied.
6. *Ibid.,* p. 13; for a similar statement by Secretary McNamara, see Hitch, *Decision-Making for Defense,* p. 27. McNamara was aware that such a "philosophy" would cause some "wrenching

strains" in the department, but he was convinced, nonetheless, of the need for it. Finally, it must be noted that while Mr. McNamara has used the terms "active" and "passive," they are not employed in the sense of the Rockefeller Committee. See Senate Committee on Armed Services, *Report of the Rockefeller Committee: Department of Defense Organization,* Committee Print, 83rd Congress, 1st Session (1953), and Hensel, "Changes Inside the Pentagon."

7. Charles J. Hitch and Roland N. McKean, *The Economics of Defense in the Nuclear Age* (Cambridge, 1960), p. 254.
8. "McNamara Defines His Job," p. 110. Emphasis supplied.
9. *Ibid.,* p. 109.
10. *Ibid.,* pp. 108-109; *Hearings,* before the Defense Subcommittee of the House Appropriations Committee, 88th Congress, 2nd Session (1964), Part IV, pp. 304-305.
11. "Address," United States Naval War College, June 6, 1963, in *United States Naval Institute Proceedings,* XC (January 1964), 153.
12. *Ibid.,* p. 152.
13. *Hearings,* House Defense Subcommittee (1964), Part IV, pp. 304-305. Emphasis supplied.
14. "Address," Naval War College, p. 158. There is no question that Enthoven's Naval War College address was part of a running controversy throughout 1963 with the Navy and with Admiral George W. Anderson, Jr., short-lived Chief of Naval Operations. The "Anderson Affair" will be examined at a later point.
15. *Ibid.,* p. 156.
16. "Address," The Aviation and Space Writers Convention, May 25, 1964.
17. For comments on this point, see Jack Raymond, *Power at the Pentagon* (New York, 1964), pp. 292-293, and James Reston, *New York Times,* April 22, 1966.
18. "McNamara Defines His Job," p. 108.
19. Enthoven, "Address," Naval War College, pp. 152, 155; and see *Hearings,* before the Joint Committee on Atomic Energy on Nuclear Propulsion for Naval Surface Vessels, 88th Congress, 1st Session (1964), pp. 159-162, and *Hearings,* House Defense Subcommittee (1964), Part IV, pp. 103, 107, 111, 363, 365-368.
20. *Economics of Defense in the Nuclear Age,* pp. 107, 118-119. Emphasis supplied.
21. *Ibid.,* p. 120. Emphasis supplied.

22. *Decision-Making for Defense,* pp. 50, 26, *et passim.* Hitch has provided a kind of "prologue" and an "epilogue" in his two works, *The Economics of Defense in the Nuclear Age* (1960) and *Decision-Making for Defense* (1965). In the preface of the former he writes that he is concerned with presenting *a new way of looking at* military problems and how to go about solving them (p. v). Later there is a significant qualification or limitation imposed on his analysis: "Our major emphasis in this volume is on peacetime preparations for war and deterring war. This means that we are interested *mainly in peacetime, not wartime costs.* We are trying to make the most of the resources available for national security in peacetime. In principle the wartime costs are relevant. In practice we can frequently ignore them. For in the case of general nuclear war, we expect the war to be fought with the forces in being at its outbreak. The major economic problem is to maximize the capability of these forces efficiently before the war starts—so efficiently that we hope an enemy will never dare to start it. In the case of limited war there may well be significant production of weapons and expenditure of resources after the limited war begins (as in the case of Korea) but occasional wars for limited objectives will cost little compared with the year-in year-out costs of peactime preparedness" (pp. 169-170; emphasis supplied). Mr. Hitch was writing before the Vietnam war! Mr. McNamara underlined some of the major axioms of the new management in his "Address" before the American Society of Newspaper Editors on June 1, 1963.

23. *Economics of Defense in the Nuclear Age,* p. 243.

24. *Decision-Making for Defense,* p. 52; *Hearings,* Subcommittee on National Policy Machinery (1961), Vol. I, p. 1194.

25. Mr. McNamara, according to one report, tired of explaining the merits of his techniques and confined himself to asserting their value; see "McNamara's Management Revolution," pp. 117ff. An excellent example of Mr. McNamara's responsiveness to "charges" against his management is "Statement by Secretary of Defense Robert S. McNamara Analysing Allegations Concerning the Readiness of United States Military Forces," *New York Times,* March 3, 1966, p. 16.

26. *Decision-Making for Defense,* p. 18.

27. *Hearings,* Subcommittee on National Policy Machinery (1961), Vol. I, pp. 1005-1006; see the identical language in *Decision-Making for Defense,* p. 23.

28. See *Hearings,* Subcommittee on National Policy Machinery (1961),

Vol. I, pp. 1221, 1064; and *Hearings,* before the House Committee on Armed Services on Military Posture, 89th Congress, 1st Session (1965), pp. 310-316. For comments of the Comptroller General of the United States Department of Defense accounting systems, see *Hearings,* before a Subcommittee of the House Committee on Government Operations, 88th Congress, 2nd Session (1964), pp. 6-13. Hitch had hoped to abandon the defense appropriations procedure of full funding of programs because this did not disclose the "time-phased" costs of such programs. His purpose was to keep track of the rate of expenditures or "resources consumed"; however, he concluded rather quickly that "accounting difficulties" precluded this approach. See *Decision-Making for Defense,* pp. 29-33, and *Hearings,* Subcommittee on National Policy Machinery (1961), Vol. I, p. 1005.

29. *United States Government Organization Manual, 1965-1966* (Washington: Government Printing Office, 1965), p. 137.
30. For a graphic flow chart of the finanacial management system, see "McNamara's Management Revolution," pp. 118-119.
31. *Decision-Making for Defense,* p. 25. McNeil has commented on Hitch's lack of knowledge of "what has been the general practice for years." Hitch recognized that Secretary Gates had introduced four-year planning projections but not cost projections. See *Hearings,* Subcommittee on National Policy Machinery (1961), Vol. I, pp. 1059-1060.
32. *Decision-Making for Defense,* p. 31; *Hearings,* Subcommittee on National Policy Machinery (1961), Vol. I, pp. 1006-1007.
33. See *Hearings,* Subcommittee on National Policy Machinery (1961), Vol. I, p. 1012.
34. *Decision-Making for Defense,* p. 32. Emphasis supplied. The phrase in italics often reads "related to missions or roles," which Hitch has stated was the point of the programming function. Missions, roles, or functions of the Department of Defense need to be kept conceptually distinct from "national security objectives." At other times the point will be made that effectiveness is simply to be related to costs.
35. *Ibid.,* p. 34; *Hearings,* Subcommittee on National Policy Machinery (1961), Vol. I, pp. 1007, 1111.
36. *Ibid.,* Vol. I, pp. 1197, 1218. When Mr. McNamara states that "in my mind, I equate planning and budgeting and consider the terms almost synonymous," he appears to be using them somewhat more broadly than does Mr. Hitch in connection with the FMS.

37. Captain Stanley M. Barnes, USN, "Defense Planning Processes," *United States Naval Institute Proceedings*, XC (June 1964), 32-33. Emphasis supplied.
38. Colonel Robert N. Ginsburgh, USAF, "The Challenge to Military Professionalism," *Foreign Affairs*, XLII (January 1964), 255. "The challenge to military expertise." says Colonel Ginsburgh, "is the most important aspect of the challenge to military professionalism because expertise is, after all, the very basis of any profession" (p. 258). Colonel William R. Kintner (USA, retired) noted early in the MaNamara administration that the most serious charge that had been raised against the Secretary of Defense had to do with the nature of his relations with the military. The exact meaning of "civilian control" had never been so ambiguous, Kintner contends. He suggested that rather than thinking of the problem in terms of "civilian control," it could be better stated as one of "proper civil-military relations." It is precisely this problem that Mr. McNamara found the least congenial. See, "The McNamara Era in the Defense Department," *Naval Review* (1962-1963), pp. 112, 120.
39. "The Challenge to Military Professionalism," p. 255. Emphasis supplied.
40. "Defense Planning Processes," pp. 29ff. Captain Barnes quotes Professor Huntington with approval: "Strategic programs, like other major policies, are not the product of expert planners, who rationally determine the action necessary to achieve desired goals. They are the result of controversy, negotiations and bargaining among officials and groups with different interests and perspectives." See Samuel P. Huntington, *The Common Defense* (New York, 1961), p. 146; see also James R. Schlesinger, "Quantitative Analysis and National Security," *World Politics*, XV (January 1963), 295-315.
41. "Defense Planning Processes," p. 31.
42. *Hearings*, Subcommittee on National Policy Machinery (1961), Vol. I, pp. 1061-1062.
43. *Hearings*, House Defense Subcommittee (1964), Part IV, pp. 305, 4.
44. See especially Hitch and McKean, *Economics of Defense in the Nuclear Age*, Ch. 9, and Hitch, *Decision-Making for Defense*, Ch. 3. Mr. Enthoven's addresses cited above (Naval War College, June 6, 1963, and Aviation and Space Writers, May 25, 1964) are at points emotional advocacy of cost-effectiveness analysis. A more studied statement, without any loss of ardor, is Alain G. Enthoven, "Systems Analysis and the Navy," *Naval Review*

(1965), pp. 98-117. Daniel Seligman has found Mr. McNamara more dogmatic than any of his subordinates. He writes that "McNamara's value judgments, expressed in the relationships he finds between costs and effectiveness, probably should be questioned more closely than they have been." But Seligman notes that no one seems to be doing so. See "The McNamara Management Revolution," p. 248.

45. E. S. Quade, "Military Systems Analysis" (RM-3452-PR), RAND Corporation, January 1963, reprinted in Davis B. Bobrow, ed., *Components of Defense Policy* (Chicago, 1965), pp. 420-438. For an excellent discussion of the "weaknesses and possible abuses, as well as the effectiveness, of an analytic approach to long-range military planning," see E. S. Quade, ed., *Analysis for Military Decisions* (Chicago, 1964). In this series of lectures, Albert Wohlstetter defines systems analysis as "an attempt to discern and answer questions of importance in choice of policy" (p. 103). This definition, it must be suggested with deference, has little heuristic utility. For a balanced critique of systems analysis, see Albert Wohlstetter, "Scientists, Seers and Strategy," *Foreign Affairs*, XLI (April 1963), 466-478.

46. "Military Systems Analysis," p. 421n. Emphasis supplied. Mr. McNamara has noted himself that, in choosing between aircraft A and aircraft B, "the basic question, first, is whether we should have either one of them." See *Hearings*, House Defense Subcommittee (1964), Part IV, p. 305.

47. "Military Systems Analysis," p. 428. Emphasis supplied.

48. "Defense Planning Processes," pp. 35-36.

49. "Military Systems Analysis," pp. 424, 434; Enthoven, "Address," Naval War College, p. 153. Quade, as a matter of fact, refers to systems analysis both as a form of art and a form of engineering. See "Military Systems Analysis," pp. 423, 439. Mr. McNamara has set the following role for cost-effectiveness analysis: "It aims to assist the decision-maker by furnishing him with quantitative estimates of the effectiveness and costs of each of the alternative courses which he could choose. Confronting a multiplicity of options we have turned to analytical techniques to assist us in our choice." See "McNamara Defines His Job," pp. 108-109. And while Hitch has pointed to limitations of cost effectiveness, he insists that it is the analytic foundation for the making of sound, objective choices by the Secretary of Defense. See *Decision-Making for Defense*, pp.

57-58. For the view of one of Hitch's colleagues at RAND, see Bernard Brodie, "The Scientific Strategists," in *Selected Papers*, compiled by the Subcommittee on National Security Staffing and Operations, Senate Committee on Government Operations, Committee Print, 87th Congress, 2nd Session (1962), pp. 190-201.

50. "Military Systems Analysis," p. 435.

51. *Hearings*, Subcommittee on National Policy Machinery (1961), Vol. I, pp. 1187, 1221-1223.

52. *Hearings*, House Defense Subcommittee (1964), Part IV, p. 221. Mr. McNamara was prepared to make revisions in the major operating commands as well, with or without the concurrence of the Joint Chiefs of Staff; see *ibid.*, Part IV, pp. 315-316. Charles J. V. Murphy commented in the spring of 1962 that while the operating commands still reported to the JCS, Mr. McNamara's control over them had become so explicit that he, rather than the Chiefs, seemed to be in direct command of the armed forces. See "The Education of a Defense Secretary," *Fortune*, LXV (May 1962), 104. For an account of the secretary's direct role in the Cuban missile crisis, see Jack Raymond, *Power at the Pentagon*, pp. 284-286.

53. The "commanders" were Charles J. Hitch (Strategic Delivery Systems), Paul H. Nitze (Limited War), Thomas D. Morris (Installations and Logistics), and Herbert F. York (Research and Development). The first two assignments caused the most concern; it was not yet clear that Mr. McNamara did not intend to establish "functional" commands for these two areas in keeping with the Symington Committee recommendations. See *Hearings*, House Defense Subcommittee (1961), Part I, pp. 57-59, 101.

54. Previously, the Deputy Director of Defense Research and Engineering had assistant secretary status. In the aftermath of the Cuban missile crisis, civilian defense was given this prominence as well. The movement of such people as Mr. Enthoven, Mr. Horwitz, and Mr. McNaughton through the office of Secretary of Defense structure suggests that Mr. McNamara was wholly prepared to impose an "influence pattern" on the table of organization. For the views of Comptroller Anthony, see his *Planning and Control Systems: A Framework for Analysis* (Boston, 1965).

55. Mr. Stahr did not want to be thought of as leaving the Pentagon with "a parting blast." Still it was evident that he considered

Mr. McNamara's management mode "overreaching." *New York Times,* July 8, 1962.

56. See "The Service Secretary: Has He a Useful Role? " pp. 471-472, 479.

57. *Hearings,* House Defense Subcommittee (1961), Part VI, p. 227, and Part III, pp. 29-32.

58. *New York Times,* June 30, 1964.

59. *Hearings,* House Defense Subcommittee (1964), Part IV, pp. 307-308; *Hearings,* Subcommittee on National Policy Machinery (1961), Vol. I, pp. 1199-1205. Emphasis supplied.

60. Title 10, Section 137 (e).

61. *Hearings,* Subcommittee on National Policy Machinery (1961), Vol. I, pp. 1199-1205; *Hearings,* before the Senate Committee on Armed Services, Military Procurement Authorization for Fiscal Year 1967, 89th Congress, 2nd Session (1966), p. 229.

62. *Ibid.*

63. *Washington Post,* April 19, 1964.

64. General Wheeler succeeded General George H. Decker as Army Chief of Staff. General Harold K. Johnson succeeded General Wheeler.

65. *Hearings,* before the Permanent Subcommittee on Investigations of the Senate Committee on Government Operations, TFX Contract Investigation, 88th Congress, 1st Session (1963), Part III, p. 781.

66. *Ibid.,* Part III, pp. 774, 780.

67. *Ibid.,* Part III, pp. 775, 783.

68. *Ibid.,* Part III, pp. 792, 780.

69. Admiral George W. Anderson, Jr., "Address," Navy League Convention, San Juan, Puerto Rico, May 3, 1963.

70. See above, pp. 69-70.

71. Admiral George W. Anderson, Jr., "Address," National Press Club, Washington, D.C., September 4, 1963.

72. *Ibid.*

73. *Ibid.*

74. *Ibid.* Anderson, in fact, presented the position paper of the Joint Chiefs of Staff on the Nuclear Test Ban Treaty to the Senate in June 1963 as well as "his own views." See *Hearings,* before the Preparedness Investigating Subcommittee of the Senate Committee on Armed Services, Military Aspects and Implications of Nuclear Test Ban Proposals and Related Matters, 88th Congress, 1st Session (1963), pp. 300ff. Mr. McNamara and General Lemnitzer discussed the "difference of opinion" between them

which arose when the secretary assigned all military space functions to the Air Force in 1961 in *Hearings, House Defense
Subcommittee* (1961), Part III, pp. 33-37.
75. *Power at the Pentagon,* p. 280. Raymond describes General Bernard
A. Schriever's speech to the Air Force Association in Philadel-
phia on September 21, 1961, as "the last major speech by a
man in uniform calling without inhibition for a military
oriented space program" (p. 238).
76. *Ibid.,* pp. 320-321. Raymond continues, "One of the dangers in the
modern and vast centralized military establishment is the reduction of controversy within the bureaucracy. Increased and centralized authority in the hands of the Secretary of Defense is an
aid to good management, but has as a drawback the possibility
that all alternatives may not reach him, that the interpretation
of facts may be tailored to his prejudices" (p. 322). Secretary of
the Air Force Eugene M. Zuckert has noted that one of the
results of the B-70 controversy was to "bring into key Air Staff
positions men who were intellectually flexible." See "The Service Secretary: Has He a Useful Role? " pp. 472-473.
77. Aaron Wildavsky, "The Political Economy of Efficiency: Cost-
Benefit Analysis, Systems Analysis, and Program Budgeting,"
Public Administration Review, XXVI (December 1966), 292-310
(especially 307-310).
78. Clark Clifford became the ninth Secretary of Defense on March 1,
1968. There is little question that he is "a political man." There
is little question that the President who appointed him was
more comfortable with such a man. The seeming rapport between the eighth Secretary of Defense and President Johnson
after the latter took office proved to be no more than that.

Notes to Chapter 3

1. *Congressional Record,* June 14, 1966 (Vol. 112, No. 97), p. 12483.
   It will be noted that the *Record* prints a slightly altered statement.
2. André Beaufre, *An Introduction to Strategy* (New York, 1965), p.
   12.
3. *Ibid.,* p. 29.
4. *Ibid.,* p. 45; also pp. 22, 136-138.
5. This was noted early from as far away as Paris by a friendly critic,
   Raymond Aron. He questioned whether Mr. McNamara was

fully appreciative of the qualitative aspects of the arms race and the strategic implications of various industrial, technological, and financial "tactics" that were open to him. See Aron, *The Great Debate* (New York, 1964), pp. 42-43, 255-256. Richard Fryklund, then military writer for the *Washington Evening Star,* stated Mr. McNamara's point of view as follows: "McNamara believes that the Eisenhower approach wasted many billions of dollars on marginal and redundant weapons. McNamara tries to get more results per dollar by developing components of possible future weapons and postponing the expensive decisions to put the components together and create weapons." *Washington Evening Star,* October 20, 1964. See also Hanson W. Baldwin, "Slow-Down in the Pentagon," *Foreign Affairs,* XLIII (January 1965), 263-264, and Jack Raymond, *Power at the Pentagon* (New York, 1964), p. 235.

6. See Jerome B. Wiesner and Herbert F. York, "National Security and the Nuclear Test-Ban," *Scientific American,* CCXI (October 1964), 27-35. For Harold Brown's concurrence in the Wiesner-York thesis, see *Hearings,* before the Preparedness Investigating Subcommittee of the Senate Committee on Armed Services, Military Aspects and Implications of Nuclear Test-Ban Proposals and Related Matters, 88th Congress, 1st Session (1963), Part II, p. 882. See also the views of Deputy Director of Defense Research and Engineering, Eugene Fubini, in *U.S. News & World Report* (August 16, 1965), pp. 61, 63.

7. See *Scientific American,* CCXI (December 1964), 8-12; *The Reporter* (August 12, 1965), pp. 47-50. The unfortunate aspect of the Wiesner-York article cited above (note 6) does not lie in its conclusions; rather there is an effort by the two authors to trade hard on their scientific standing to make a putative scientific argument. The argument is not an example of "science." The apolitical structure of Wiesner's thought is seen in the following: "The hope for disarmament in a context of acute distrust between powerful nations *lies in solutions to the problem of inspection"* (emphasis supplied). See Wiesner's "Inspection for Disarmament," in Lewis J. Henkin, ed., *Arms Control: Issues for the Public* (Englewood Cliffs, N.J., 1961), p. 140.

8. See *Hearings,* before the Senate Committee on Foreign Relations, Nuclear Test-Ban Treaty, 88th Congress, 1st Session (1963), pp. 99, 103-115, 151-159. The following year Mr. McNamara told the House Defense Subcommittee that he favored the treaty because it "will serve to reduce the possible diffusion of nuclear

202 *Notes to pp. 103-139*

weapons." See *Hearings,* before the House Defense Appropriations Subcommittee, Department of Defense Appropriations for 1965, 88th Congress, 2nd Session (1964), Part IV, p. 323. One of the trenchant observations of Raymond Aron is that accurate estimates of military strength are dubious. See *The Great Debate,* pp. 210-211.

9. See Klaus Knorr and Oskar Morgenstern, *Science and Society (Some Critical Thoughts on Military Research and Development),* Policy Memorandum No. 32, Center for International Studies (Princeton, 1965), pp. 21, 35; see also Charles J. Hitch, *Decision-Making for Defense* (Berkeley, 1965), pp. 43-44, 72-73. Some may note a "built-in bias" against new weapon systems on Hitch's part in Charles J. Hitch and Roland N. McKean, *The Economics of Defense in the Nuclear Age* (Cambridge, 1960), pp. 172-173.

10. See *Hearings,* before the House Defense Appropriations Subcommittee, Department of Defense Appropriations for 1962, 87th Congress, 1st Session (1961), Part IV, p. 41, and *Hearings,* before the Subcommittee on Naional Security and International Operations of the Senate Committee on Government Operations, The Atlantic Alliance, 89th Congress, 2nd Session (1966), Part VI, pp. 186-191. For an excellent general discussion, see Henry A. Kissinger, *The Troubled Partnership* (New York, 1966).

11. *Statement* of Secretary of Defense Robert S. McNamara before the House Armed Services Committee on the Fiscal Year 1966-70 Defense Program and the 1966 Defense Budget, February 18, 1965, pp. 37-38.

12. See *Hearings,* before House Defense Appropriations Subcommittee, Department of Defense Appropriations for 1961, 86th Congress, 2nd Session (1960), Part I, p. 26. Harlan B. Moulton, writing from the vantage point of the Arms Control and Disarmament Agency in 1964, states that "one of the most important changes made by Secretary McNamara in the nation's general war strategy was to predicate all planning on the basis of a second strike posture." Whether this represented a change and whether counterforce and damage limitation had the priority that Moulton suggests is extremely doubtful. Indeed, the evidence is that Mr. McNamara was an eclectic at best and indecisive at worst in the matter of a general nuclear war strategy. See Harlan B. Moulton, "The McNamara General War Strategy," *Orbis,* VIII (Summer, 1964), 238-254.

13. See *Hearings,* before House Defense Appropriations Subcommittee,

Department of Defense Appropriations for 1965, 88th Congress, 2nd Session (1964), Part IV, p. 26.

14. *Statement* of Secretary McNamara, February 18, 1965, pp. 42-43.

15. See *Hearings*, before the House Armed Services Committee on Military Posture, 89th Congress, 2nd Session (1966), p. 7333.

16. *Statement* of Secretary McNamara, February 18, 1965, p. 48.

17. *Hearings*, House Armed Services Committee (1966), p. 7356; *Statement* of Secretary McNamara, February 18, 1965, p. 62.

18. See *Hearings*, before Senate Armed Services Committee and Defense Appropriations Subcommittee, Military Procurement Authorizations for Fiscal Year 1967, 89th Congress, 2nd Session (1966), pp. 253-254; also *Hearings*, House Defense Subcommittee (1960), Part VI, pp. 32-33.

19. See *Hearings*, before the House Armed Services Committee on Military Posture, 89th Congress, 1st Session (1965), p. 484; *Statement* of Secretary McNamara, February 18, 1965, pp. 50-51; Bill Davidson, "Can Nike X Save Us?" *The Saturday Evening Post* (August 27, 1966) 19-21; Roswell L. Gilpatric, "Our Defense Needs," *Foreign Affairs*, LXII (April 1964), 366-378. However, the House Minority Leader, Congressman Gerald R. Ford of Michigan, has expressed concern about the McNaughton thesis; see *Hearings*, House Defense Subcommittee (1964), Part V, pp. 56-63.

20. *Hearings*, House Armed Services Committee (1966), p. 7339.

21. *New York Times*, March 29, 1961, p. 16. For a general treatment of this theme, see Robert W. Tucker, *The Just War: A Study in Contemporary American Doctrine* (Baltimore, 1960), and also James M. Roherty, "On Success in War: A Note on Murray's Argument," *Orbis*, V (Fall 1961), 360-366.

22. *Hearings*, House Defense Subcommittee (1961), Part I, pp. 6-7; Samuel P. Huntington, *The Common Defense* (New York, 1961), pp. 268ff.

23. Aron, *The Great Debate*, p. 79. Even William W. Kaufmann, whose book *The McNamara Strategy* is an unabashed effort in behalf of the Secretary of Defense (see the reviews by S. L. A. Marshall in *United States Naval Institute Proceedings* [March 1965] and Bernard Brodie in *World Politics* [July 1965], suggests that "the missile gap had evaporated" and that, "contrary to the expectations of 1960," the United States had acquired upon Mr. McNamara's coming into office in 1961 "a strategic nuclear capability which was superior to that of the Soviet Union in numbers, in quality, and in survivability." Mr. Kaufmann would give credit

to Secretary McNamara, however, for "a quick fix" during 1961. See *The McNamara Strategy* (New York, 1964), pp. 65-72 especially. Deputy Secretary of Defense Roswell L. Gilpatric spoke in October 1961 of "tens of thousands" of nuclear delivery vehicles with "more than one warhead for each vehicle." "Address," Business Council, Hot Springs, Virginia, October 10, 1961.

24. *Hearings,* House Defense Subcommittee (1961), Part III, pp. 7-10, 139-140. In this, his first budget presentation, Mr. McNamara displayed some doubt about precise statements of military strength. These doubts tended to wane in succeeding years.

25. *Hearings,* House Armed Services Committee (1965), pp. 1117-1118. Secretary McNamara had testified during the Nuclear Test-Ban Treaty hearings that he saw no requirement for a nuclear weapon in the 60- to 100-megaton range such as the Soviet Union apparently had developed. He stated, instead, a preference for "two, or three smaller weapons." If the secretary meant to suggest by this nuclear warheads in the 25- to 35-megaton range, these would be weapons deliverable by aircraft. In any event, the burden of General McConnell's observation is that the "heavy" weapons must be delivered by manned systems. See *Hearings,* Senate Foreign Relations Committee (1963), pp. 100-102. James R. Schlesinger wrote in 1965 that the number of strategic delivery vehicles had remained virtually constant during Mr. McNamara's tenure, but that more importantly the amount of "deliverable megatonnage" had decreased 50 percent; see *The Reporter* (August 12, 1965), p. 49.

26. *Hearings,* House Armed Services Committee (1965), p. 211.

27. See Eugene M. Zuckert, "The Service Secretary: Has He a Useful Job?" *Foreign Affairs,* XLIV (April 1966), 472-473; *Hearings,* House Armed Services Committee (1965), pp. 372-373. It is not the purpose of this study to delve into the "TFX Contract Case"; it is still too early to determine what the "payoff" of this decision will be. However, it needs to be emphasized that no decision made by Secretary McNamara is more exclusively his own than this one. Whatever the "payoff," it is Mr. McNamara's.

28. See *New York Times,* August 18, September 20, and September 22, 1964; *Washington Evening Star,* August 20, 1964; *Hearings,* House Armed Services Committee (1965), p. 369; *Statement* of Secretary of Defense Robert S. McNamara before Subcommittee Number 2 of the House Armed Services Committee on the

Fiscal Year 1967-71 Strategic Bomber Program, January 25, 1966, p. 17 (emphasis supplied). For an extended discussion of the identity of "we," see the *Congressional Record,* June 14, 1966, pp. 12456-12461.

29. See *Hearings,* House Defense Subcommittee (1961), Part III, pp. 494-495.
30. *Ibid.,* Part III, p. 409.
31. *Hearings,* House Defense Subcommittee (1964), Part IV, pp. 494-495.
32. *Ibid.,* Part V, p. 58.
33. *Ibid.,* Part V, p. 103.
34. *Ibid.,* Part IV, pp. 471, 491. Emphasis supplied.
35. *Ibid.,* Part IV, pp. 32-33.
36. *Ibid.,* Part IV, pp. 516-518.
37. *Ibid.,* Part IV, pp. 472, 533-534.
38. See, for example, the testimony of General Thomas S. White at *Hearings,* before the Subcommittee on National Security and International Operations of the Senate Committee on Government Operations, Conduct of National Security Policy, 89th Congress, 1st Session (1965), Part II, pp. 81, 87, and the testimony of General Bernard A. Schriever and General John P. McConnell at *Hearings,* before Subcommittee Number 2 of the House Armed Services Committee, Department of Defense Decision to Reduce the Number and Types of Manned Bombers in the Strategic Air Command, 89th Congress, 2nd Session (1966), pp. 6100ff.
39. *Hearings,* House Defense Subcommittee (1961), Part IV, pp. 29-33.
40. See "Our Defense Needs," p. 373.
41. See "The Service Secretary: Has He a Useful Role? " pp. 472-473.
42. *Hearings,* House Defense Subcommittee (1961), Part III, p. 454.
43. *Hearings,* House Armed Services Committee (1965), p. 490.
44. *Ibid.,* pp. 586-594.
45. *Hearings,* Subcommittee Number 2 of the House Armed Services Committee (1966), p. 6097.
46. *Ibid.,* p. 6101.
47. *Ibid.,* p. 6172.
48. *Ibid.,* pp. 6205-6209.
49. *Hearings,* before the Joint Committee on Atomic Energy, Nuclear Propulsion for Naval Surface Vessels, 88th Congress, 1st Session (1963), p. 41. Hanson Baldwin has called Brown "a remarkably unadventurous scientist"; see "Slow-Down in the Pentagon," p. 267. One may note how Brown mixes personal premises and

technical judgment in his testimony on the Nuclear Test-Ban Treaty. See *Hearings,* Senate Foreign Relations Committee (1963), pp. 550ff.; also *Hearings,* House Defense Subcommittee (1964), Part V, pp. 56-63 and 43-45.

Notes to Chapter 4

1. A singular account of the Pacific confrontation is, of course, Samuel Eliot Morison, *History of United States Naval Operations in World War II,* 15 vols. (Boston, 1947-1962). See especially Vols. I and XII-XIV. Among "official reports," see *U.S. Naval Aviation in the Pacific* (Washington: U.S. Navy Department, 1947), and Fleet Admiral Ernest J. King, USN, *U.S. Navy at War, 1941-1945: Official Reports to the Secretary of the Navy* (Washington: U.S. Navy Department, 1946). Two works among many biographies and memoirs are of particular value: Admiral Frederick C. Sherman, USN, *Combat Command: The American Aircraft Carriers in the Pacific War* (New York, 1950), and E. P. Forrestel, *Admiral Raymond A. Spruance, USN* (Washington, 1966). Finally, Clark G. Reynolds, *The Fast Carriers* (New York, 1968), is also recommended.

2. See especially Vincent Davis, *Postwar Defense Policy and the U.S. Navy, 1943-1946* (Chapel Hill, N.C., 1966), and Paul Y. Hammond, "Super Carriers and B-36 Bombers: Appropriations, Strategy and Politics," in Harold Stein, ed., *American Civil-Military Decisions* (Montgomery, Alabama, 1963), pp. 465-564. Hammond's study is a good summary of opinion among ranking naval officers in the aftermath of the war. There has been, however, a considerable evolution of thought about the role of carriers since that time with most of the change occurring in the 1960s. The "Forrestal literature" should also be consulted; see notes to Chapter 1.

3. See text, pp. 161-162.

4. On the need for the Navy to continually develop doctrine, especially with respect to the attack carrier, see Carl H. Amme, Jr., "Crisis of Confidence," *United States Naval Institute Proceedings,* XC (March 1964), 26-35, and Admiral David L. McDonald, USN, "Carrier Employment Since 1950," *United States Naval Institute Proceedings,* XC (November 1964), 26-33.

5. At the same time, the Navy would be compelled to retain the F8U (CRUSADER) in the inventory through the 1960s. So long as

ESSEX class carriers served in an attack carrier role, without deck or elevator capacity to operate F4's, the lighter F8U would serve as a first-line air-superiority fighter.

6. This theme is seen particularly in the small work of George Fielding Eliot, *Victory Without War, 1958-1961* (Annapolis, 1958), and in his "Our Far-Flung Ramparts," *United States Naval Institute Proceedings*, XC (October 1964), 26-34. More generally it is found in the following: William R. Braisted, *The United States Navy in the Pacific, 1897-1909* (Austin, 1958); O. J. Clinard, *Japan's Influence on American Naval Power, 1897-1917* (Berkeley, 1947); Bernard Brodie, *Seapower in the Machine Age* (Princeton, 1941); George T. Davis, *A Navy Second to None: The Development of Modern American Naval Policy* (New York, 1940); J. C. Vinson, *Parchment Peace: The U.S. Senate and the Washington Conference, 1921-1922* (Athens, Georgia, 1955); Jeter A. Isley and Philip A. Crowl, *The U.S. Marines and Amphibious War: Its Theory and Its Practice in the Pacific* (Princeton, 1951); Nicholas Spykman, *America's Strategy in World Politics* (New Haven, 1942); and Harold and Margaret Sprout's works, *The Rise of American Naval Power, 1776-1918* (Princeton, 1939), *Toward a New Order of Sea Power: American Naval Policy and the World Scene, 1918-1922* (Princeton, 1940), and *Foundations of National Power* (Princeton, 1946). This wholly incomplete list may be described as a gloss on the works of Alfred Thayer Mahan. The theme is persistent and fundamental in American strategic and, particularly, naval thought, yet Secretary McNamara does not evidence familiarity with it.

7. The "lay prejudice against bigness in naval vessels" is exemplified in the position taken by Secretary McNamara. For his views on the "vulnerability" of carriers, see note 48, below, and for those of Harold Brown see note 59 below. For an especially concise discussion of the "desirable characteristics" of an attack carrier, see the testimony of Captain Roger Mehle, USN, given to the Defense Subcommittee of the House Appropriations Committee on January 18, 1960; *Hearings*, before the Subcommittee of the House Committee on Appropriations, Department of Defense Appropriations for 1961, 86th Congress, 2nd Session (1960), Part II, pp. 55-66.

8. This is especially noted by Morison, *History of United States Naval Operations in World War II*; see especially Vols. XII-XIV.

9. The NAUTILUS (SSN 571) joined the fleet in the first administration

of Eisenhower (September 30, 1954) and had been authorized in the final year of the administration of President Harry S. Truman.

10. The House first proposed an oil-fired frigate, then changed it to nuclear propulsion. Again the following year, the House appropriated funds for a nuclear-powered frigate that had not been requested. In January 1964, the Secretary of Defense cancelled the fiscal year 1963 DLGN because of a lagging TYPHON missile system that was to be part of its armament.

11. See *Hearings,* House Defense Subcommittee (1960), Part I, pp. 60-61, 12-13. See below for similar testimony by Secretary of the Navy Fred Korth and Chief of Naval Operations Admiral George Anderson given as late as 1962.

12. See James M. Roherty, "Science, Civilians and the Military," in *Science and Society,* The Thomas Jefferson Faculty Lectures (Williamsburg, 1965), pp. 89-112.

13. Interview with Admiral Arleigh Burke, USN (retired), Chief of Naval Operations, 1955-1961.

14. For Admiral Anderson's statement on February 8, 1962, see *Hearings,* before the House Armed Services Committee on Military Posture, 87th Congress, 2nd Session (1962), pp. 3630-3631, and for Secretary Korth's statement on February 28, 1962, see *Hearings,* before the Subcommittee of the Senate Appropriations Committee, Department of Defense Appropriations for 1963, 87th Congress, 2nd Session (1962), pp. 205-206. The tenor of the testimony is exactly that of Secretary Gates' in 1960.

15. I have associated Admiral Burke with this point of view on the basis of interview notes (see note 13 above) and on the basis of testimony he gave in his final appearance as Chief of Naval Operations before the Defense Subcommittee of the House. See *Hearings,* before the Subcommittee of the House Appropriations Committee, Department of Defense Appropriations for 1962, 87th Congress, 1st Session (1961), Part III, pp. 382-387. I must report that Admiral Burke takes exception to this conclusion; however, the author can put no other interpretation on his remarks. Finally, the author does not wish to imply that what he takes to be Admiral Burke's view is not on occasion a necessary one.

16. Admiral Rickover has made his views well known. In addition to his testimony before the Joint Committee on Atomic Energy in October 1963 (see below), see the following: *Hearings,* before

the Subcommittee of the House Appropriations Committee, Department of Defense Appropriations for 1965, 88th Congress, 2nd Session (1964), Parts III and V, especially Part III, pp. 397ff.; *Hearings,* before the Joint Committee on Atomic Energy, Naval Nuclear Propulsion Program, 89th Congress, 2nd Session (1966); and *Hearings,* before the Subcommittee of the House Appropriations Committee Department of Defense Appropriations for 1967, 89th Congress, 2nd Session (1966), Part VI.

17. *Hearings,* before the House Armed Services Committee on Military Posture, 89th Congress, 2nd Session (1966), p. 8084.

18. See note 14 above. Admiral Rickover made clear to the Joint Committee on Atomic Energy why he thought the Navy had been caught short on the question of CVA-67: "In my opinion the Navy has been derelict in not taking the initiative to figure out what the Navy should be like and for this reason the Department of Defense has taken the initiative and the Navy has been put behind." See *Hearings,* before the Joint Committee on Atomic Energy, Nuclear Propulsion for Naval Surface Vessels, 88th Congress, 1st Session (1963), p. 99.

19. See note 10 above.

20. *Hearings,* Joint Committee on Atomic Energy (1963), pp. 63ff.

21. *Ibid.,* pp. 11-12.

22. *Ibid.,* pp. 80-81. Emphasis supplied.

23. *Ibid.,* p. 63.

24. *Ibid.,* p. 230.

25. *Ibid.,* p. 81. Emphasis supplied.

26. *Ibid.,* p. 231. Emphasis supplied.

27. *Ibid.,* pp. 231-233.

28. *Ibid.,* p. 240.

29. *Ibid.,* pp. 104-107.

30. *Ibid.,* p. 171. Emphasis supplied.

31. *Ibid.,* pp. 244-245.

32. *Ibid.*

33. *Ibid.,* p. 4.

34. *Ibid.,* pp. 4-5. Emphasis supplied.

35. *Ibid.,* pp. 245-246.

36. *Ibid.,* pp. 25-26.

37. *Ibid.,* p. 5. Admiral David L. McDonald would recount later that indeed Secretary McNamara had made up his mind prior to the Joint Committee hearings: "he made the decision in late October . . . we were unable to convince the Secretary" (on the

basis of the two studies). See *U.S. News & World Report*, LVI (March 2, 1964), 69-70.

38. *Hearings,* Joint Committee on Atomic Energy (1963), p. 25. It will be noted that Harold Brown, then Director of Defense Research and Engineering, used precisely the same language in making the same point in his testimony before the Joint Committee. *Ibid.,* pp. 34 and 39.

39. *Ibid.,* p. 70.

40. *Ibid.,* pp. 69-70. See also *Hearings,* House Defense Subcommittee (1964), Part IV, pp. 678, 719-720.

41. *Hearings,* House Defense Subcommittee (1964) Part IV, p. 206.

42. *Ibid.,* Part IV, p. 374. It was later established that "the proper number" was thirteen.

43. *Hearings,* Joint Committee on Atomic Energy (1963), p. 163.

44. *Hearings,* House Defense Subcommittee (1964), Part III, p. 405.

45. "Address," by the Honorable Paul H. Nitze, Secretary of the Navy, Joint Session of the National War College and Industrial College of the Armed Forces, March 16, 1964; reprinted in *United States Naval Institute Proceedings,* XC (July 1964), 160-166.

46. *Hearings,* Joint Committee on Atomic Energy (1963), p. 163. Emphasis supplied.

47. *Ibid.,* p. 185. Emphasis supplied.

48. *Ibid.,* pp. 180 and 186. Emphasis supplied.

49. *Ibid.,* p. 173.

50. *Ibid.,* pp. 163 and 171.

51. *Ibid.,* p. 178.

52. *Ibid.,* p. 177.

53. *Report,* of the Joint Committee on Atomic Energy, Nuclear Propulsion for Naval Surface Vessels, 88th Congress, 1st Session (1963), pp. 12ff. and pp. 28ff.

54. *Hearing,* Joint Committee on Atomic Energy (1963), pp. 177-178, 190.

55. *Ibid.,* pp. 190-191.

56. *Ibid.,* p. 41.

57. *Ibid.,* p. 34.

58. *Ibid.,* pp. 132, 137-138, and 141.

59. *Ibid.,* pp. 132-133.

60. *Ibid.,* pp. 39-42, 142-144.

61. *Ibid.,* pp. 38-39.

62. *Ibid.,* p. 52.

63. *Ibid.,* pp. 38-39.

64. *Ibid.,* pp. 56-59, 120-125.

65. *Report,* Joint Committee on Atomic Energy (1963), p. 3. Emphasis supplied.
66. *Ibid.,* p. 4.
67. *Ibid.,* pp. 4-5.
68. *Ibid.,* p. 5. More than two years later, the Joint Committee indicated that it was more than ever convinced that the Secretary of Defense had erred. See *Hearings,* before the Joint Committee on Atomic Energy, Naval Nuclear Propulsion Program, 89th Congress, 2nd Session (1966), pp. iii-vii.
69. *Report,* House Committee on Appropriations, Department of Defense Appropriation Bill, 1965, 88th Congress, 2nd Session (1964), p. 37.
70. *Hearings,* House Defense Subcommittee (1964), Part IV, p. 206.
71. *Hearings,* before the Joint Committee on Atomic Energy, Nonproliferation of Nuclear Weapons, 89th Congress, 2nd Session (1966), pp. 80-81.
72. *Hearings,* House Armed Services Committee (1966), pp. 7471-7472.
73. *Hearings,* before the House Armed Services Committee on Military Posture, 89th Congress, 1st Session (1965), p. 324.
74. *Ibid.,* p. 710.
75. *Hearings,* House Armed Service Committee (1966), pp. 7471-7472.
76. See Luther J. Carter, "Nuclear Carriers: Studies Convince the Skeptics," *Science,* CLI (March 18, 1966), 1368-1371.
77. *Hearings,* House Armed Services Committee (1966), pp. 7878-7902.
78. *Ibid.,* p. 7472.
79. Rear Admiral Henry L. Miller, USN, while Commander of Carrier Division Three on "Yankee" station, prepared a document which summarized the Navy's position on the basis of Vietnam experience: "Advantages of Nuclear Power and Its Utilization in a Combat Environment." See *Hearings,* House Armed Services Committee (1966), pp. 8023-8028.
80. *Hearings,* House Armed Services Committee (1965), pp. 526ff. and 944ff.; *Hearings,* House Armed Services Committee (1966), pp. 8078 and 8081. In October 1965, the Chief and Deputy Chief of the Bureau of Ships (Rear Admirals William A. Brockett and Charles A. Curtze) resigned. The resignations were due in part to the degree of control exercised by the office of the Secretary of Defense over the Bureau of Ships in the Department of the Navy. See *New York Times,* October 28, 1965.

Index